Handicapped Children
in Residential Care

...dy of Policy Failure

also published by the Bedford Square Press:

Aids and adaptations (LSE)
Holes in the welfare net

Handicapped Children in Residential Care

A Study of Policy Failure

Ann Shearer

BEDFORD SQUARE PRESS | NCVO

First published 1980 by the
BEDFORD SQUARE PRESS of the
National Council for Voluntary Organisations
(formerly The National Council of Social Service)
26 Bedford Square London WC1B 3HU

ISBN 0 7199 1035 8

Printed in England by Henry Ling Ltd, at the
Dorset Press, Dorchester, Dorset

Acknowledgements

This study would not have been started without the interest of James Loring, until recently director of the Spastics Society, who found some of the financial support I needed. My thanks to him, and to the Equity and Law Charitable Trust, for their own contribution.

The work would have proved more difficult without the libraries of the Home Office, Department of Education and, particularly, Department of Health and Social Security. My thanks to their staffs for their help and hospitality.

The statutory data is reproduced with the permission of the Controller of Her Majesty's Stationery Office.

The study would have been far weaker without the comments of Peter Moss and the late Professor Jack Tizard, of the Institute of Education, London University, on an early draft. My thanks to them for their time and trouble. Neither they, nor anyone other than myself, of course, bears any responsibility for the final version.

Ann Shearer

Contents

Tables

Introduction

The Children Act of 1948 set up a system of caring for children not able to live in their own homes which was radically different from anything which had been on offer for them before. That system was recommended by the Curtis Committee on the care of children; its report has ever since been seen as something of a blueprint for official enquiries. The Committee took evidence, visited, was shocked by what it found and made sweeping recommendations for change. A new pattern of child care was the result and it is a pattern on which services for most children who are not able to live with their own families are still based.

But for handicapped children in search of a substitute home, there have been very different and often very inferior developments. While some severely physically handicapped children have gone to boarding schools, others have gone to live in long-stay hospitals. For most of the severely mentally and multiply-handicapped children, what we now know as mental handicap hospitals have offered the only alternative home to their family one. Over thirty years after the Curtis Committee reported on the shocking state of child care, there are still children living away from their own families in conditions as shabby and insensitive to their need for warmth, affection and stimulation as the orphanages ever were.

This report does four things. It traces the development of these very different types of care for different categories of children, by looking at the overall picture and at what the official aims of government departments involved in the residential care of children have been. It does not tackle the important questions of why children have lived away from their own families and whether they should have done; it is about what was meant to happen to them and what did happen when they did. It doesn't look at all children living away from home either: it leaves out those in community homes with education (what used to be called approved schools) and in places set up for children with mental illness, because these settings raise complicated questions about 'treatment' which I didn't feel able to take on board.

The report also looks at the quality of care in different settings and tries to tease out some of the reasons why this care is good or bad. It tries to explain why, when child care in general changed so fundamentally after 1948, the residential care of children categorised as handicapped did not and has not since. And finally, the report offers some suggestions on what we should be doing now to ensure that all children, whatever their label, are offered the same basic standards of care.

For the past thirty years, child care policy has simply not touched many handicapped children in residential care. The principles on which child care in general has been founded have been trickling through in official pronouncements on what ought to be happening for handicapped children since the end of the 1950s. But very little has been done to translate these principles into action. For a start, there has been neither the machinery to do this nor, it seems, the will to create the machinery. Ever since 1948, children in the official care of local authorities have had the protection of specific legislation. Most handicapped children living away from home have not, because they are not officially 'in care'. They have come under either education legislation, which has little to do with child care, or mental health legislation, which has less. The effect in both cases has been to separate them from the mainstream of policy towards children away from their own homes. In 1979, children in the care of local authorities were under one division of the Department of Health and Social Security, while those with physical handicaps were under a second and those with mental handicaps under another again – the last two dealing with policies for handicapped adults as well.

This legal and administrative muddle is an expression of something deeper – the attitudes this society holds towards people, both adults and children, who are handicapped.

Handicapped people pose a great number of problems for societies like ours, which believe in efficiency, production, making money and moving fast to cram in as many experiences as possible. Those we categorise as handicapped may be inefficient, slow, non-productive and poor, and we wrap up these characteristics in a packet called 'social problem'. Our traditional solutions to this problem have been procrustean: we have expected disabled people to fit the norms of society as a whole. We have increasingly been able to offer them help to adapt – corrective surgery, aids and appliances, support to their families, special educational techniques. It is when people do not then fit into normal social patterns that we are stumped. What we have most often produced for these obstinate misfits are 'holding operations' – residential establishments which care for them until they die. Rather than question the ways in which society has failed to adapt to their needs, we categorise these people as 'chronically sick' and so excuse ourselves from having to do more than ensure that the medical profession has taken over. It is only in recent years that society has begun to adapt its public buildings, its work processes and its housing to people with disabilities, rather than writing them off as 'incurable' if they themselves cannot do all the adapting.

We have taken the same approach to handicapped children. Since 1944, it has been accepted that children should go to ordinary schools if they can fit into these. It has also been increasingly accepted that children with handicaps and in need of care away from their own homes should come into the regular child care system if they can fit into it. But the assumption is still that it is the children and not the systems which must do the adapting. It is only with recent interest in, for example, fostering severely handicapped children and opening units for them in ordinary schools that a few authorities are beginning to challenge the accepted patterns.

More often, our approach to severely handicapped children has been coloured by assumptions about their adulthood. Instead of seeing children who need sometimes very specialised help, we see the shadow of adults who have not received that help and assume that the children, whatever we do, must grow up in that mould. The enormous increase in special schooling since the war has been designed to help handicapped children to grow up able, as far as possible, to share normal opportunities. But it has also separated them very early in their lives from those opportunities, and this is sometimes justified on the grounds that in any case they will never, realistically, be able to use those opportunities. The assumption that severely mentally handicapped children should be cared for in hospital wards which are very different from the accepted pattern of child care has been fed by assumptions about their 'inevitable' future in the adult wards across the campus. One of the most important principles the Curtis Committee established for children in care was that what they were offered should no longer be coloured by the assumption that they would inevitably grow up to be domestic servants or army recruits: they had a right to a childhood and not just to a training for adulthood. This right has not yet been recognised for all severely handicapped children.

These attitudes to children who are handicapped have been at the back of much professional and official thinking over the past thirty years. The Curtis Committee itself both reflected the attitudes of its day and set the tone for the future. It had the ideal chance – and one which has never been repeated – to look at the conditions of *all* children living away from their homes. It very quickly excluded those with handicaps from more than a passing glance because, it said, most of their problems, particularly the medical aspects, were outside its terms of reference. (1) Ever since, children with handicaps have been clearly segregated in the professional mind. The volumes of research abstracts on child care do not include the studies on handicapped children; these are in a separate volume. The British Association of Social Workers has brought out a Charter of Rights for children in care, but it has not turned its attention to the particular problems of handicapped children living away from home. (2) The Newsom and Plowden Reports on secondary and primary education did not tackle special schools. (3) It was more than a decade later that the concept of special education got its first thorough airing since 1889. (4) The Seebohm Report on the personal social services, for all its emphasis on integration, made most of its recommendations for mentally handicapped children in a chapter which bracketed them not with other children, but with mentally handicapped and mentally ill adults. (5)

So children with handicaps have been segregated from professional and official thinking about children as a whole. If they are mentally handicapped in particular, they have also because of the legislation under which they fall been bracketed with the adults they might become. The major post-war study of mental handicap hospitals made little distinction between the needs of adults and children in this form of residential care. (6) Official government enquiries into abuses in these hospitals have echoed this overall approach to 'the mentally handicapped' as a group. (7) At its worst, this bracketing of children with adults has meant that the children are barely considered at all. The Personal Social Services Council, for instance, in its recent work on the purpose and nature of residential care, excluded all children except those with mental handicaps; in the event, it barely considered the children at all. (8)

It is against this background that the different types of residential care for differently categorised children have developed since the Curtis Committee made its report. Lady Allen called the pamphlet of evidence she collected for the Committee 'Whose Children?' because so many agencies were involved with them that in the end none was really responsible for them. For many handicapped children, particularly those with mental and multiple handicaps, the same question could be asked today.

Notes

1 *Report of the Care of Children Committee* (Curtis Report), Cmd. 6922, HMSO, 1946.

2 'Children in Care – a BASW Charter of Rights', *Social Work Today*, vol. 8, no. 25, 29.3.77.

3 *Half our Future: a Report of the Central Advisory Council for Education (England)*, Ministry of Education, HMSO, 1963; *Children and their Primary Schools: a Report of the Central Advisory Council for Education (England)*, DES, HMSO, 1967.

4 *Special Educational Needs. Report of the Committee of Enquiry into the Education of Handicapped Children and Young People* (Warnock Report), Cmnd. 7212, HMSO, 1978.

5 *Report of the Committee on Local Authority and Allied Personal Social Services* (Seebohm Report), Cmnd. 3703, HMSO, 1968.

6 Morris, P., *Put Away*, Routledge and Kegan Paul, 1969.

7 *Report of the Committee of Inquiry into Allegations of Ill-Treatment of Patients and Other Irregularities at Ely Hospital, Cardiff*, DHSS, Cmnd. 3975, HMSO, 1969; *Report of the Farleigh Hospital Committee of Enquiry*, DHSS, Cmnd. 4557, HMSO, 1971; *Report of the Committee of Inquiry into South Ockenden Hospital*, HMSO, 1974; *Report of the Committee of Inquiry into Normansfield Hospital*, DHSS, Cmnd. 7357, HMSO, 1978.

8 Personal Social Services Council, *Residential Care Reviewed*, 1977.

1 Curtis and its conclusions

On July 15, 1944, *The Times* carried a letter from Lady Allen of Hurtwood, calling for a public enquiry into the 'largely uncivilised territory' of child care. 'The public', she said,

'are for the most part unaware that many thousands of these children are being brought up under repressive conditions that are generations out of date and are unworthy of our traditional care for children. Many who are orphaned, destitute or neglected still live under the chilly stigma of "charity"; too often they form groups isolated from the main stream of life and education, and few of them know the comfort and security of individual affection.'

Lady Allen knew what she was talking about. She had spent much of the war setting up children's nurseries; she had visited many children's homes. The response to her letter was immediate and enormous. Letters poured into *The Times* from professional people and others who had grown up under the system, who agreed with her, and from people who ran children's homes, who said that there was nothing to worry about. The House of Commons was alerted, members began to ask questions and an enquiry was announced on December 7.

At the beginning of 1945, public interest in children living away from home was given a powerful impetus by the death of Dennis O'Neill while he was being fostered with his brother in Shropshire, and by the conviction of his foster-father for manslaughter. The abuses to which these children had been subjected were horrifying; it turned out that neither of the local authorities involved with them had visited them for nearly six months before Dennis's death. There was something clearly wrong with the boarding-out system, then. And with the publication of *Whose Children?*, culled by Lady Allen from the personal letters she had received from people who had lived through childhood in care as well as worked in children's homes, it became clearer than ever that there was a great deal wrong with this system, too.

The membership of the Committee of Enquiry, with Myra Curtis, principal of Newnham College, Cambridge, in the chair, was announced at the end of February. (1) The Committee started work the following month:

'to inquire into existing methods of provision for children who, from loss of parents or from any cause whatever are deprived of a normal home life with their own parents or relatives; and to consider what further measures should be taken to ensure that these children are brought up under conditions best calculated to compensate them for the lack of parental care'. (2)

If the system the Committee was to look into was positively harmful to many of the children who had to live with it, it also had all the administrative confusion that could be expected from such a piecemeal jumble of provision, complicated by the turmoils of the war. Lady Allen had found the whole thing a 'super-colossal muddle' when she tried to sort out which government departments were responsible for which children. The Curtis Committee was to echo her findings, if in a more sober tone. 'It would not be difficult,' it said at the end of its work, 'to find children similar in type and circumstance whose treatment has been quite different merely because they have been dealt with by different departments under different statutes'. (99)* The Ministry of Health and the Home Office, for instance, each had its own set of rules for boarding-out, and these did not tally. Understandably, the Committee reported that the division of responsibilities was seen by local authorities and others as 'confusing and tending to imperfect administration'. (429)

The largest number of children who were not living in their own homes were officially 'destitute'. The majority were maintained by the Poor Law, under which local authorities had a duty to provide relief and 'set [them] to work or put [them] out as apprentices'. In theory none of these children were allowed to live in public assistance institutions except in emergencies or unless they were ill; in fact, a good number found themselves there. Most, though, were in local authority homes – which could be either large 'barracks', grouped 'cottage homes', each with between ten and thirty children, or 'scattered homes'. The other large category of destitute children found themselves in voluntary homes – which took in some Poor Law children for local authorities as well. A relatively small number were boarded out.

The second large group of children living away from home was made up of those who were categorised as delinquent or in need of care or protection. Many of these children were in approved schools; others were in local authority or voluntary children's homes, or were fostered. Apart from these two major categories of child, there were others who were fostered for reward under public health legislation, or fostered while waiting for adoption. Finally, there were two groups who were peculiar to their time – homeless evacuees and war orphans. With the exception of the last, who were the responsibility of the Ministry of Pensions, most of these children were under the Ministry of Health, through a plethora of Acts, of which the most important was the Poor Law Act of 1930. But the Home Office was responsible for voluntary homes as well as the lives of children categorised as delinquent or in need of care or protection (under the Children and Young Persons Acts of 1933 and 1938). While destitute children who were also handicapped could find themselves in homes or hospitals under the Ministry of Health or Home Office, others could end up in special boarding schools under the Ministry of Education (Education Act 1944). Finally, children certified as 'mentally defective' and 'ineducable' were the responsibility of a

---

*Numbers in italic in brackets refer to paragraphs in the *Report of the Care of Children Committee*, HMSO, 1946.

different agency altogether – the Board of Control, set up under the Mental Deficiency Act of 1913 and responsible for mentally handicapped and mentally ill children and adults. In theory, all children certified by the Board should have been in 'certified institutions' run by local authorities and under its control. In fact, because of the shortage of these, large numbers were still in public assistance establishments approved by the Board to take them. Large but unknown numbers of mentally handicapped children who had not been certified were also in these public assistance institutions as well as in unapproved workhouses and children's homes; the Board of Control had nothing to do with them. (3) Table 1 gives Curtis's own figures for the number of children in all these different settings.

Table 1

CHILDREN DEPRIVED OF A NORMAL HOME LIFE, 1946

England and Wales, thousands

Category of child	Local authority institutions*	Special schools	Voluntary homes and hospitals	Foster homes	Approved schools & remand homes & probation homes	TOTAL
Destitute	23.4		29.3	4.9		57.6
Homeless evacuees	1.9		.3	3.0		5.2
Maintained for reward				10.7		10.7
Pending adoption				2.4		2.4
Delinquent/ in need of care or protection	2.0		2.0	6.0	13.4	23.4
Mentally disordered/ handicapped	7.0		.3	.2		7.5
Physically/ mentally handicapped		14.5				14.5
War orphans				3.6		3.6
TOTAL	34.3	14.5	31.9	30.8	13.4	124.9

*including 6,500 in public assistance institutions:16,900 in children's homes: the rest unspecified

Source : Cmnd. 6922, Table IV

The brief of the Curtis Committee was to look at the lives of all these children, whatever their intelligence, whatever administrative arrangements they came under, and to establish a new system of care for them all. As the Committee itself underlined : 'This is the first enquiry in this country directed specifically to the care of all children deprived of a normal home life and covering all groups of such children.' There has never been the chance for such a comprehensive look at the care of children since.

The Committee's findings

The Committee visited establishments caring for some 30,000 children and reckoned to have taken a 'good sample' of each kind or care. *(101)* Members visited children who were boarded out, and children in public assistance children's homes and nurseries, public health nurseries, private and voluntary children's homes, hostels for working boys and girls and probation hostels, approved schools and remand homes ; they also went to 14 institutions and homes for 'defective' children, 5 long-stay children's hospitals, 2 institutions for the deaf and dumb, 2 sanitorium schools, 2 crippled children's homes, 3 homes for blind babies and a home of recovery for sick children.

Overall, the Committee concluded that the defects of these homes 'were not of harshness, but rather of dirt and dreariness, drabness and over-regimentation. We found no child being cruelly used in the ordinary sense, but that was not perhaps a probable discovery on a casual visit. We did find many establishments under both local authority and voluntary management in which children were being brought up by unimaginative methods, without opportunity for developing their full capabilities and with very little brightness or interest in their surroundings. We found in fact many places where the standard of child care was no better, except in respect of disciplinary methods, than that of say 30 years ago ; and we found a widespread and deplorable shortage of the right kind of staff, personally qualified and trained to provide the child with a substitute for a home background. The result in many Homes was a lack of personal interest in and affection for the children which we found shocking.' *(418)*

Within this overall picture, of course, there were extremes which were both very good and very bad. One nursery, under the administration of a Poor Law Institution, 'had sunk to the lowest level of child care which has come to our notice.' There were thirty-six children in this nursery, eight of them sick and nursed in a small ward next to the infirmary for adults, in which were 'aged and chronic sick', a mentally handicapped child and one with chicken pox.

'In the children's ward was an eight year old mentally defective girl, who sat most of the day on a chair commode, because, the nurses said, 'she was happy that way'. She could not use her arms or legs. There were two babies with rickets clothed in cotton frocks, cotton vests and dilapidated napkins, no more than discoloured cotton rags. The smell in this room was dreadful. A premature baby lay in an opposite ward alone. This ward was very large and cold. The healthy children were housed in the ground floor corrugated hutment which had been once the old union casual ward. The day room was large and bare and empty of all toys. The children fed, played and used their pots in this room. They ate from cracked enamel plates, using the same mug for milk and soup. They slept in another corrugated hutment in old broken black iron cots some of which had their sides tied up with cord. The mattresses were fouled and stained. On inquiry there did not appear to be any available stocks of clothes to draw on and it was said by one of the assistant nurses that 'everything was at the laundry and did not come back'. The children wore ankle length calico or flannelette frocks and petticoats and had no knickers. Their clothes were not clean. Most of them had lost their shoes ; those who possessed shoes had either taken them off to play with or were wearing them tied to their feet with dirty string. Their faces were clean ; their bodies in some cases were unwashed and stained.' (*144*) As soon as the Committee spoke to the local authority about the state of these children, they were removed to a separate nursery.

It was not uncommon in public assistance institutions (PAIs) for 'defective' children to be mixed in with others, and this was something which exercised the Committee particularly. There was an additional hazard in these places ; in one, 'the matron said she could do nothing with the older children to prevent them from wandering all round the premises and that she had reported to the Public Assistance Officer that they might be associating with adult defectives.' (*147*)

In one PAI, 100 years old, the Committee found 27 children, between six months and fifteen years old, including 12 infants, half of whom were still being nursed by their mothers.

'In the same room in which these children were being cared for was a Mongol idiot of gross appearance for whom there was apparently no accommodation elsewhere. A family of five normal children aged about six to sixteen, who had been admitted on a relieving officer's orders, had been in the institution for ten weeks. This family, including a boy of 10 and a girl of 15, were sleeping in the same room as a three year old hydrocephalic idiot, of very unsightly type, whose bed was screened off in the corner.'

In this institution, they were told, 'children were occasionally sent back to the homes in which they had been neglected because it was thought better for them than the conditions under which they would have to be cared for in the workhouse'. (*140*) These conditions were not unique ; such were the conditions in other institutions that there too, 'normal children were sleeping with low grade mentally defective children'. (*142*)

The Committee was in no doubt about what it thought of these arrangements.

'It is clear that defective and epileptic children and occasionally children suffering from mental illness, constitute a serious problem in the children's wards of institutions. The staff are not qualified to deal with them, they are a disturbance in the care of normal children and the adult wards to which they are sometimes moved are equally unsuitable for them.'

It gave three instances of administrative delay which had deprived children of the care and training which they should have been receiving under the Mental Deficiency Acts. (*149*) But its real concern was not with them. 'Possibly of more serious import is the presence of defective and sometimes uncontrollable children with those who are normal.' And it gave an example to drive home the point, from a ward of twenty-two very young children:

9

'There were four children between the ages of five and eight. One was a girl, a blind epileptic in bed, she was quite helpless and had been there for about three years in the same ward as the normal children. There was a boy aged eight in a cot who was obviously a low grade mental defective. He hardly ever kept his clothes on, but kept tearing them off. He was in the same ward as the normal children with a screen round him, but he could be seen behind the screen. He had been there since April 1943 and was now kept in bed all the time. He was there because apparently accommodation for him could not be found anywhere else. There was also an epileptic child of four, who was said to be totally incontinent and helpless. He was permanently bed-ridden.' (*150*)

Public assistance children's homes had the same problem, if not to the same degree, in the 'considerable numbers of dull and defective children' they were accommodating. In two cottage homes visited were groups of children certified as 'feebleminded' and going to a special day school 'owing to the lack of accommodation for them in a residential special school' ; the medical officer of one of these homes said they were 'not suitably catered for in Homes intended for normal children'. In another home, the eldest of a family of three 'defective' children was said to be disturbing other children because of her sexual behaviour ; but she was being kept on for the time being 'to help in the Home'. (*216*)

When it assessed institutions which catered specifically for mentally or physically handicapped children, the Committee was careful, from the start, to make clear its own lack of expertise. 'We have considered the residential accommodation for children deprived temporarily or permanently of home life by reason of physical or mental infirmity or deficiency, but have regarded the medical treatment of such children as outside our scope.' (*5*) It was aware, it said, that the 'care, training and education of mentally defective children is a matter requiring knowledge', but felt that its observations justified comments on 'certain points'. (*327*) It seemed to feel on surer ground when it came to institutions for physically handicapped children.

'The purpose of our visits was not to assess the medical care... but to estimate as well as we could the conditions under which many of the children spent long years of their childhood and the sort of occupations, interests and contacts which were provided for them. Insofar as the hospital or home had for long periods to take the place of the natural home, we were anxious to see how far it was able to supply any substitute for the part played by family care in the child's development.' (*337*)

The Committee found great variations in the standards of accommodation specifically for mentally handicapped children. One Convent home for eighty girls aged fourteen and over, 'compared with the surroundings of many of the children described... in this report,... was outstanding in its effort to provide a happy place for these unfortunate girls'. The girls learned embroidery, leatherwork and rug-making and dressmaking, among other crafts ; they often acted in plays produced by the sisters and there was a film projector in the home ; the rooms and furnishings were pretty and bright. (*333*) By contrast, in one local authority home there seemed to be nothing for the children to do except housework and in another for fourteen 'educable' children 'the living rooms were few and dark, the bedrooms rather better, the kitchen dark and neglected with ragged oilcloth on the table. There was only one bath for fourteen boys in the home in which frequency of bathing is obviously desirable. There was no sign of comfort, little decoration and no pictures in the playroom.' (*328*) In another local authority institution, however, which catered for fifty boys and fifty girls together with a larger number of adults (what would today be called a mental handicap hospital), the children's villas were more recently built than the old workhouse which made up the main building, and were 'well designed, spacious, widely separated and with ample ground... The whole place seems well-cared for, it is light and attractive.' (*328*) In this or a similar institution, the care and training was 'imaginative', with a 'school' for some children (although in theory they were all 'ineducable'), scouts and guides and dormitory lockers for personal possessions. (*333*)

The Committee was impressed by the 'physical comfort and surroundings' of the children in the orthopaedic hospitals it visited, although 'it was unusual to see any attempts to make the ward attractive to the children by means of curtains, paint or other decoration'. Teachers worked in all the hospitals and in two the children had good leisure activities and an obviously interested and loving staff. In a third, when the Committee members visited at four in the afternoon :

'The children were lying on their beds, mostly awake. One or two had picture books or dolls but others had nothing and looked bored. A young nurse was in charge and did not seem much interested in discussing the welfare or occupations of the children. It seemed that these children had little of occupational or social interest after the teacher left... We were told that there were two occupational therapists in the hospital, but that they did not have anything to do with the children who were receiving education.' (*341*)

The sanitorium schools presented an even starker contrast. The first, with 180 tubercular children, had a full educational programme and seemed 'a remarkable place. The children did not appear to be sick children and even the most deformed were lively and intelligent.' The second housed twenty-two children in 'decayed wooden huts which had been condemned before the war' ; the children had been there for two years, although they were due to move soon. The accommodation had twice been condemned as 'rat-ridden and unsafe', heating and lighting were 'altogether out of date', the decoration dreary and the children, making allowance for all their handicaps, seemed 'remarkably backward'. There was an

'obvious need for some form of occupation to fill the gap between the limited hours of schoolroom education and the children's long hours of entire leisure which the few nurses could not hope to deal with. The children seemed to have few toys and little or no materials for play or handwork ; they were bored and listless. It was clear to us that the nursing staff and the teacher were struggling with almost impossible conditions.' (345)

The two homes for deaf and dumb children the Committee visited were both 'large and barrack-like in appearance and old-fashioned in furnishings, though both were set in beautiful grounds'. In one at least the atmosphere was happy and the education seemed careful and thorough. 'But we regretted that this group of children, already so isolated from other children and from the world, could not be housed in more modern buildings with a more homelike and comfortable appearance. When it is remembered that these children spend the whole period of their childhood in these Homes except for holidays, the need for comfort and brightness is apparent.' (342)

Finally, the two homes for crippled children and the home of recovery seemed almost idyllic, with a high standard of education and impressive staff. 'We wish that some of the lessons which had evidently been learned in the care of these severly handicapped children could have been passed on to those in charge of homes for normal children.' (343) The home of recovery was, quite simply, 'one of the most delightful of any kind which we saw'. (346)

The Committee's recommendations

The Committee saw well the dangers of institutional life for children, 'the tendency to a lack of interest in the child as an individual and to remote and impersonal relations'. However good the material standards – and the Committee had seen standards that were often better than children would have at home –

'we are convinced... that, on the human and emotional side, they continually feel the lack of affection and personal interest... the longing for caresses from strangers, so common among little children in Homes, is in striking and painful contrast to the behaviour of the normal child of the same age in his parents' home. The lack of the mother's fondling cannot of course be entirely made good, but something must be provided which gives the child the feeling that there is a secure and affectionate personal relation in his life.' (477)

For the large majority of children not living in their own homes, the Committee made detailed and sweeping recommendations to provide that something. There should, for a start, be a new local authority department, with a childrens' officer as its executive, to take charge of them ; they should be the responsibility of a single government department instead of being scattered through the bewildering number of different departments as they had been in the past. (430–2, 434, 435, 441, 444, 446) Boarding out was the favoured substitute for a child's own home, and should, the Committee said, be greatly expanded. (*461, 465*) For children who could not be boarded out, there should be family group homes, with a maximum of twelve places, either 'scattered' or grouped together, and each under the charge of houseparents. (*478, 485–7*) There should be special reception homes and residential nurseries for children under two and a half. (*478, 482–4*) The homes should be near the centre of urban or village life and children should go to local schools unless the home was so big that it needed its own school ; children should have their own possessions and dress like others of their age ; contact with friends should be encouraged ; and there should be plenty of recreational opportunities in the homes. (*493*)

Although the Committee had clearly seen many things which were less than good in the care of mentally and physically handicapped children, its recommendations for their future were extremely sparse compared to these detailed and careful proposals for 'normal' children. In spite of its original brief to look at the conditions of *all* children not living in their own homes, it drew its own boundaries to exclude this minority. 'The mentally or physically handicapped child', it said, 'presents different problems, most of which, and in particular the medical aspects, are outside our terms of reference.' (*508*) As far as mentally handicapped children were concerned, the Committee contented itself with proposals for making sure that they would not in future mix with others as they had in the past. It recommended an immediate census of 'ineducable' children in public assistance institutions and children's homes and that 'the earliest possible steps be taken with a view to providing for them in properly staffed Homes or Colonies'. (*509*) It would be the duty of the children's officer to refer to the Mental Deficiency Committee any child under two she suspected of being mentally handicapped and to bring to the notice of the Education Committee any child over that age she thought might need special educational treatment or be ineducable. There should be no changes in the present administrative structures for mentally handicapped children, although 'special attention' should be paid to private establishments for retarded children who were placed by local authorities some distance away. (*510–11*)

The Committee also singled out two other groups of children in need of special attention. The first were epileptic and delinquent or epileptic and unstable ; because of their dual handicap these children fell between different provisions and ended up in children's homes or lived for years in workhouses because no one else would take them. Their numbers were so small that regional or national provision could be made for them. The second group ended up in mental hospitals, not because they were mentally ill, but because of 'violent tempers, sex delinquency, larceny or wandering'. Alternative provision should be found for them immediately ; at the least they should be cared for 'in a way which would not bring them into contact with adults suffering from mental illness'. (*513*)

Finally, in spite of its recognition that institutions were in fact substitute homes for many physically handicapped children, the only recommendation the Committee made for them had to do with educational and recreational opportunities. The Ministry of Health, it said, should urge on all local authorities the importance of arranging education for all children in hospital 'and the employment of skilled workers on the recreational side'. If the child was in care, the children's officer should make sure that he or she was getting all the proper opportunities. (*514*)

In sharp contrast to the changes it wanted to see for normal children in care, then, the Committee proposed no more than a tinkering with existing arrangements for children with handicaps. It accepted completely the current administrative arrangements for handicapped children living away from home and the attitudes that went with them ; it had very little to say about the vital constituents of a substitute home for these children. Its most far-reaching recommendation for them, that mentally handicapped children should move to 'properly staffed homes or colonies', was not original. The Committee itself quoted the Wood Report of 1929 in support of its case : 'The number of institutions... is totally inadequate and must be increased, especially when regard is had to the far larger number of children who, in our view, should be notified in the future.' (4) By 1946, this was no more than received wisdom.

This recommendation, in fact, offers the best illustration of the separation in the Committee's mind between normal and 'defective' children. For the first group, it had been adamant that children's homes should be completely separated from adult institutions. Even the then current proviso that children could go to these places for up to six weeks in an emergency should, it said, be withdrawn – apart from babies with their mothers. Children should only ever be received into workhouses for twenty-four hours. (*48*) By recommending that mentally handicapped children should be sent to 'colonies' – the specialist local authority institutions – it was quite deliberately sending them to institutions with a mixed population of children and adults. Its proposal that children in care suspected of having a mental handicap should be referred to the Mental Deficiency Committee set the seal on their separation from others in care. It even separated them from children with physical handicaps, with whom, Curtis said, the children's officer should keep in touch if they went to hospital.

One of the Committee's main concerns had been with the quality of care children received ; clearly no administrative changes could create the sort of life it wanted children in care to have without the right kind of staff. So concerned had the Committee been about this that it had issued an interim report on the importance of training. (5) In its main report, it even laid down minimum staff ratios. (*493*) And yet, in spite of considerable evidence of grave staff shortages in homes and institutions for mentally handicapped children, (*329*) it had nothing to say to the Board of Control about these. It had reservations about the staffing of one home for blind babies it visited : 'We left it with some doubt about a purely hospital training for those who are to have the entire charge of the children... There was great efficiency and much real kindness, but warmth of affection and motherliness seemed lacking.' (*344*) But it had nothing to say about the child care component of residential life for handicapped children. Once more, it seems that the Committee accepted completely that the way these children lived was the way they must live, that the residential care they received was somehow part of that 'treatment' which it took to be outside its terms of reference. Interestingly, however, the people responsible for the care and treatment of children classified as delinquent exercised no such absolute authority in the Committee's mind. Although it saw it as no part of its business to meddle with questions of criminal justice, it nevertheless felt able to make recommendations about staffing and educational emphasis in approved schools, and even about whether older girls should be sent to them at all. (*497–9*)

For the children who were to come under the care of the proposed children's departments the Committee knew what it wanted to see.

If the substitute home is to give the child what he gets from a good, normal home it must supply –

(i) Affection and personal interest ; understanding of his defects ; care for his future ; respect for his personality and regard for his self-esteem.

(ii) Stability ; the feeling that he can expect to remain with those who will continue to care for him till he goes out into the world on his own feet.

(iii) Opportunity of making the best of his ability and aptitudes, whatever they may be, as such opportunity is made available to the child in the normal home.

(iv) A share in the common life of a small group of people in a homely environment.

Some of these needs are supplied by the child's own home even if it is not in all respects a good one ; it is a very serious responsibility to make provision for him to be brought up elsewhere without assurance that they can be supplied by the environment to which he is removed. (*427*)

Just how we have set about achieving these standards for different groups of children living away from their own homes is what the rest of this report is about.

Notes

1 Allen, M. and Nicholson, M., *Memoirs of an Uneducated Lady*, Thames and Hudson, 1975.

2 *Report of the Care of Children Committee* (Curtis Report), Cmd. 6922, HMSO, 1946.

3 *ibid.*, section 1 for information on the pre-1948 pattern of child care.

4 *Mental Deficiency Committee : Report of the Joint Committee of the Board of Education and Board of Control*, Part I, General, HMSO, 1929.

5 *Training in Child Care : Interim Report of The Care of Children Committee*, Cmd. 6760, HMSO, 1946.

2 What happened next?

The main proposals of the Curtis Committee became law with the Children Act of 1948. Under this, local authorities set up children's committees, with a children's officer as chief executive, to look after all children in care. The Home Office became responsible for these children ; its inspectors visited both local authority and voluntary homes. The Act set a framework for children in the care of local authorities which was to last for over twenty years.

For other children living away from home, though – the ones the Curtis Committee had decided were outside its terms of reference – the mixture of provision was much as before. The approved school system continued under the Home Office for some twenty years for those classed as delinquent. Handicapped children, if classed as 'educable' under the Education Act of 1944, could end up in special boarding schools. Those classed as 'ineducable' because of their mental handicap continued to come under the Board of Control for more than a decade ; if they didn't live at home, they went to the 'colonies' which in 1946 became part of the provision of the National Health Service and were eventually renamed 'mental subnormality hospitals'. Some children with physical handicaps continued to live in long-stay hospitals.

So the patterns of care for children living away from their own homes could be very different, according to how they were categorised and above all according to whether they were classed as handicapped or not. And overall, the numbers of children away from home have continued to rise throughout the last thirty years.

Table 2 gives an estimate of the number of children away from home in the categories with which this report is concerned – those in the care of local authorities in foster homes and children's homes, those in homes for handicapped children, in special boarding schools, and in different sorts of hospitals – rather than taking the comprehensive look which Curtis did at all children away from their own homes. A word of caution : some of the figures are very crude estimates, based on very scanty official ones. The total is probably a fairly serious underestimation.

All through the last thirty years, however – and especially since the beginning of the 1970s – there have been attempts to bring the very different patterns of care closer together, in the context of greater co-operation between health, education and social services and a growing concern that wherever possible people should get the services they need in their own community.

There have been two approaches to this integration. The first tries to bring general health, education and social services to people who have been excluded from them. Three Acts of this sort have been particularly important

Table 2

CHILDREN DEPRIVED OF A NORMAL HOME LIFE, 1949–76

England and Wales, thousands

Children	1949	1951	1956	1961	1966	1971	1976
in local authority care							
in children's homes	24.5	25.2	21.6	19.5	19.9	22.5*	28.4*
fostered	19.3	24.3	27.1	29.1	31.8	30.2	33.1
in voluntary homes	6.0	6.6	4.6	3.6	4.9	5.5	4.2
in accommodation for the handicapped	1.3	1.9	2.2	2.0	2.1	2.3	2.8
other	4.1	4.6	6.8	5.6	5.9	6.5	7.5
in special boarding schools	11.7	14.1	20.1	20.2	20.8	21.2	21.2
in homes for the handicapped	NA	NA	NA	.5	1.0	2.0**	2.0**
in mental handicap hospitals*,****	6.0	7.0	8.0	7.0	6.5	6.4	3.8
in other hospitals	6.0	5.0	5.0	4.0	2.0	1.5	1.5
TOTAL	78.9	88.7	95.4	91.5	94.9	98.1	104.5

* community homes, excluding those with education

** England only

*** children up to 15 only, 1949–66, up to 16, 1971–7 ; the fact that this cut-off is used for them, rather than 18, as for children in care, is an indication of how they are viewed

****children in hospital for more than 3 months

Sources :

Annual Reports, Ministry of Education and Ministry of Health, 1949, 1951

Report of a survey of long-stay hospital accommodation for children, DHSS 1970

See also Tables 3, 4, 6, 7, 8, 10

to children living away from home (as well as to others who are not) :

1 **Mental Health Act 1959.** This followed the recommendations of the 1957 report of the Royal Commission on Mental Illness and Mental Deficiency, by abolishing the Board of Control and bringing people categorised as mentally ill or handicapped into the regular health services ; the Ministry of Health (and later the Department of Health and Department of Health and Social Security) became directly responsible for the hospitals they lived in and local health authorities were given powers to provide community care for them, including junior and senior training centres and hostels or residential homes.

2 **Education Act 1970.** Children who had been excluded from the educational system because their mental handicap categorised them as 'ineducable' were finally brought into its scope ; their training centres became a new kind of special school – 'educationally subnormal (severe)'.

17

3 **Children and Young Person's Act 1969.** This abolished the legal notion that children who needed local authority care and those who had got into trouble with the law were two different species. Children in the second category as well as the first became the responsibility of local authorities. Approved schools were abolished as a separate category and became part of the provision of local authority and voluntary 'community homes' ; regional planning committees were set up to weld the old children's homes and approved schools into the new, single system.

Only the third of these measures has really closed many gaps between different categories of children living away from their own homes – and even there, 'community schools with education' (the old approved schools) are still a distinct category among children's homes. Severely mentally handicapped children in special boarding schools are still under the Education Act rather than any legislation that deals with the care of children away from home – unless they are also 'in care'. Even if mentally handicapped children live in local authority hostels, these hostels are still governed by the Mental Health Act and not the children's legislation which governs community homes.

The second approach to integration of services has been a more general one, born of a realisation that the often arbitrary divisions between health, education and social services may get seriously in the way of bringing help to people who need it. The need to bring these services closer together has been talked about a great deal during the 1970s – it is unusual to go to any meeting and not have 'multi-disciplinary teamwork' and 'joint care planning' ringing in your ears by the end of it. Three measures have helped this integration become more real :

1 **Social Services Act 1971.** This brought together all social services to children, families, the elderly and the disabled under newly-created social services departments of local authorities, following recommendations of the Seebohm Committee, which reported in 1968. For children in local authority care, this meant the end of the children's departments and of the Home Office's responsibility ; services for these children, including community homes, are now run by social services departments (and some voluntary agencies) and overseen by the Department of Health and Social Security. The departments also took over residential and other provision for mentally ill and handicapped people from local health departments, though homes for them – whether children or adults – are still governed by the 1959 Mental Health Act.

2 **National Health Service Reorganisation Act 1974.** This created a new way of managing the NHS, but it also set up health areas which usually have the same boundaries as local authorities – which in theory at least should make joint-planning of services easier.

3 **Joint-financing.** This was introduced in 1976/7, to encourage health and social services departments to work together to create schemes for people like the elderly and the disabled of all ages who had ended up in the

hospital service because there was no local authority provision for them. Under this scheme, health authorities can put up the capital costs of a project and help local authorities with running costs for a specified period. The scheme is a small one – £8m in the first year, £21m for 1977/8, and a projected £40m for 1980/1 – but it begins at least to redirect resources from the hospitals to local community services.

Again, none of these measures have done anything to change the legal position of children living away from their own homes or the administration under which they find themselves. They have simply helped to offer a framework under which services to these children – particularly if they are severely handicapped – can come closer together. This has been seen increasingly as essential if they are to get the help they need. The Seebohm Committee, for instance, made a great deal of the need for co-operation between its proposed social services departments and health and education authorities. (1) Both the Court Committee on the child health services and the Warnock Committee on special education have since echoed its concern. (2,3). Legislation has developed and recommendations have been made against a growing acceptance of a philosophy of 'community care'. The concept is still a woolly one : some people take it to mean that care should be offered to people at home, by family and neighbours ; others think that it means these 'carers' should have the help of statutory authorities ; others again take community care to include residential homes and institutions which are small and local rather than large and distant from the people they serve ; yet others include locally-based hospital services under the general rubric. But the general message seems clear enough : people should get the help they need as near as possible to their own homes and if they have to leave these homes, the substitute should be as near to the real thing as possible in the opportunities it offers.

These principles have been part of services to children for many years. The 1948 Children Act was the first statute to give local authorities a specific duty to work towards returning children to their own homes. The 1963 Children and Young Person's Act gave them powers to help children in their own families and so stop them coming into care at all and this has been an accepted part of social work with children ever since. The basis of the Seebohm proposals was 'a community-based and family-oriented service which will be available to all'. Children, it said, should be helped as far as possible within the context of their family, the community in which they live or to which they will return and the schools they attend (4). Services to handicapped children have been based on the same principles ; home, it is generally agreed, is the best place for them to be whenever possible, or at least some local substitute. 'Community care' for people classed as mentally ill or handicapped – both adults and children – was a major theme of the Royal Commission on Mental Illness and Mental Deficiency. More recently, the Court Committee's proposals for district handicap teams were designed to

19

offer parents the help they needed to keep their child at home. (5) (For a summary of the main legislation and official reports from 1948 to 1979 which have affected children living away from home, see the Appendix.)

Whatever the philosophy, however, the fact remains that more and more children are actually living away from their family homes. The fall in the number living in hospital has been outweighed by the rise in the number in special boarding schools.

What has been the intention of services to these children, and what have they actually been offered ? The next chapters look at official attitudes to children in the care of local authorities, children in special boarding schools and in different sorts of long-stay hospitals, together with what sort of framework for living they have been offered.

Notes

1 *Report of the Committee on Local Authority and Allied Personal Social Services* (Seebohm Report), Cmnd. 3703, HMSO, 1968.

2 *Fit for the Future : Report of the Committee on Child Health Services* (Court Report), Cmnd. 6684, HMSO, 1976.

3 *Special Educational Needs. Report of the Committee of Enquiry into the Education of Handicapped Children and Young People* (Warnock Report), Cmnd. 7212, HMSO, 1978.

4 Seebohm Report, paras 2,189.

5 Court Report, paras 7.35 –8.

3 Children in care

As the Curtis report made plain, the children's departments which started in 1948 hardly inherited much on which to build a service. But they not only constructed this service with remarkable dispatch ; they incorporated into it ever-rising numbers of children. Table 3 shows the growth of the service over twenty years.

The 1969 Children and Young Person's Act, as we have seen, replaced the 1948 system with one which welded together provision for children in care

Table 3

CHILDREN IN THE CARE OF LOCAL AUTHORITIES, 1949–70

England and Wales, thousands

	1949	1951	1956	1961	1966	1970
TOTAL IN CARE	**55.2**	**67.7**	**62.3**	**62.2**	**69.2**	**71.2**
Boarded out	19.3	24.3	27.1	29.1	31.8	30.3
Lodgings/ residential employment	NA	NA	2.3	1.8	1.8	1.7
Children's homes :						
reception homes		1.1	1.4	1.6	1.9	2.3
residential nurseries		4.8	4.4	3.4	3.0	2.5
homes less than 12 children	24.5	19.3	4.1	5.3	7.1	8.5
other homes			11.7	9.2	7.9	7.3
Voluntary homes	6.0	6.6	4.6	3.6	4.9	5.4
Accommodation for handicapped children	1.3	1.9	2.2	2.0	2.1	2.2
Hostels	0.7	0.8	1.1	1.0	1.0	1.2
Under charge & control of parent, guardian, relative, friend	NA	NA	NA	2.4	4.4	6.4
Other accommodation	3.4	3.8	3.4	2.8	3.1	3.4
BY AGE GROUP						
Under 2	3.9	4.2	3.6	4.3	5.8	4.5
2–5	7.8	8.9	7.5	7.5	9.5	9.1
Compulsory school age	36.0	39.6	38.7	36.9	39.2	43.2
Over compulsory school age	7.6	10.0	12.5	13.5	14.6	14.4

Sources :
Work of the Children's Department. Sixth Report, HMSO, 1951
Social Trends, No. 1, HMSO 1970
'Children in Care, England and Wales', Cmnd. 4559

and those in trouble with the law. Table 4 shows how this new pattern developed over its first six years.

Although the total number of children in care has risen dramatically, this has been because children have been staying in care longer during the 1970s. Admissions to care have in fact been tending to go down. Table 5 gives an idea of admissions over the past thirty years.

The children's departments followed the Curtis recommendations fairly faithfully in the way they cared for these growing numbers of children. Boarding out was, the Home Office advised in 1951, 'the best way of providing for a large number of children in care'. (1) In that year, a third of the children cared for by local authorities were boarded out, compared with some 29% when Curtis reported. This proportion rose steadily to a peak of 52% in 1963, at which point the Home Office warned that it could not be

Table 4

CHILDREN IN THE CARE OF LOCAL AUTHORITIES, 1971–77

England and Wales, thousands

	1971	1972	1973	1974	1975	1976	1977
TOTAL IN CARE	**87.0**	**90.8**	**93.0**	**95.9**	**99.0**	**100.8**	**101.2**
Boarded out	30.2	29.9	29.8	30.7	31.9	33.1	34.3
Lodgings/residential employment/hostels	3.2	4.1	3.8	3.5	2.7	2.5	2.3
Community homes :							
with observation and assessment	3.9	4.2	4.8	4.8	5.3	5.0	5.0
with education	7.7	6.7	7.0	6.7	6.2	6.8	6.4
residential nurseries	2.1	2.3	2.2	2.1	2.0	1.9	
other homes	16.5	16.6	17.1	19.4	21.0	21.5	22.3
Voluntary homes	5.5	5.7	5.6	5.2	4.3	4.2	3.8
Accommodation for handicapped children	2.3	2.3	2.5	2.7	2.7	2.8	2.9
Under charge of parent, guardian, relative, friend	12.3	15.2	16.1	16.6	18.0	18.0	18.0
Other accommodation	3.3	3.8	4.1	4.2	4.9	5.0	6.2
BY AGE GROUP							
Under 2	4.4	3.8	4.0	3.9	4.0	4.0	
2–5	9.0	8.3	8.6	7.9	8.3	8.4	11.8
Compulsory school age	49.9	51.9	59.3	63.6	66.9	68.1	65.9
Over compulsory school age	24.1	26.6	21.3	20.5	19.9	20.2	23.4

Sources :
Social Trends No.7, HMSO, 1976, Table 2.16
Social Trends No.8, HMSO, 1977, Table 3.6
Social Trends No.9, HMSO, 1979, Table 3.7
'Children in Care, March 1977', HMSO

Table 5

ADMISSIONS OF CHILDREN TO CARE, 1951–77

England and Wales, thousands

1951	1956	1961	1966	1969	1972	1973	1974	1975	1976	1977
36.6	38.1	45.2	54.5	51.3	53.4	53.6	52.7	51.6	52.4	52.1

Sources :
Social Trends, No.1, HMSO, 1970, Table 53
Social Trends, No.8, HMSO, 1977, Table 3.7
'Children in Care, March 1977', Table 8

expected to go on increasing indefinitely : there were children who could be better cared for, because of temperament or previous experience, in a children's home. (2) The percentage of children boarded out began to fall from then on, to 48% in 1970 ; by 1977 it was about a third.

The new departments had inherited an embarrassing stock of unsuitable old buildings. The Home Office was clear that these should be got rid of, and it was clear too on what it wanted to see in their place. And again, authorities showed a fair dispatch in following its line. By 1963, 400 of the 1500 homes, hostels, nurseries and reception centres had been used for the care of children before 1948. Three years later, the number was 352 out of 1577. (3)

In 1951, the Home Office was saying that family group homes of not more than twelve children were 'generally accepted' to be the best way of providing for children who could not be boarded out – although it qualified this four years later with the rider 'always provided that the right staff can be found and that they settle and provide the continuity of care which is especially important for the children in a small family group'. (4) Table 3 shows the growth in the number of children in these homes. By the time the children's departments were abolished, the average size of a children's home was fifteen places. (5)

If the Home Office was concerned about the size of living group in which children found themselves, it was also worried about large clutches of children living on the same site. In 1951, it was saying of grouped cottage homes – which the Curtis Committee had found housing over 7000 children –

'although it is possible within the cottages to create a family atmosphere, one of the defects of this type of care is that cottages form in the aggregate a large community of children in care, who are too numerous to be absorbed readily into the ordinary life of the neighbourhood. Where a home has facilities in the grounds such as swimming baths and playing fields, and in particular if there is a school, the isolation may be accentuated, since the children have less reason to go outside.'

Local authorities were urged to use these homes as far as possible for children in care for only a short time, and as nurseries and reception homes 'since children in these categories are less in need of outside contacts'. (6)

23

Finally, the large institutions – and the largest housed 480 children – were an 'embarrassing legacy to authorities anxious to develop the care of children on modern lines'. Those which wanted to invest in these bleak places were advised to put the minimum 'consistent with the well-being of the children' into structural alterations and to concentrate instead on improving staff ratios and furnishings – both of which could be transferred to new buildings when these became available. The fact that old buildings were unsuitable was not a reason to pour money into them ; it was a reason to increase boarding out. The Home Office felt this so strongly that it repeated its 1951 advice again in 1955. (7)

The residential nurseries attached to what had now become national assistance institutions – the old workhouses – were another problem. 'The position cannot be regarded as satisfactory until all the institutional nurseries have been cleared', the Home Office said in 1951. (8) In that year, there were seventy-four of these places ; four years later there were twelve. Table 3 shows that although the number of young children coming into care continued to rise until the abolition of the children's departments, the numbers in residential nurseries continued to fall. This was chiefly due to the large increase in fostering of young children – a trend which, as Table 4 shows, has continued into the 1970s.

A couple of examples will give some notion of how the new children's departments went about the business of constructing the new service. Lancashire County Council, one of the two authorities which already had a children's committee before Curtis reported, had over 1000 children in care in 1946 ; the county itself had two homes for 100 children and 200 more were in public assistance institutions ; fewer than 300 were fostered. Within the first two years of the department's life, from 1946–8, some 400 children were found foster homes. Four years later, 23 smaller homes had been opened, and by 1955 there were also 13 family group homes ; the number of children boarded out was nearly 1000. (9)

In neighbouring Cheshire, the number of children in care rose from 425 in 1947 to some 900 in 1954. Six new homes for a total of 230 children were approved in 1948 and two years later, the authority provided 12 homes. There was some doubt about whether family group homes were needed, but by 1953 the committee had decided to provide 16 of them, none for more than 6 children. In the first seven years of the service, the number of children boarded out rose from about 200 to 550. (10)

Progress in setting up the new service was not, of course, uniformly steady across the country. In 1950, for instance, the proportion of children boarded out varied in county boroughs from 9% to 68% and among county councils from 11% to 73% – compared to 29% throughout the country when Curtis reported. Even neighbouring authorities could go about building their service in different ways. East Sussex, which had inherited an old workhouse with 110 places, decided in 1950 that it could never offer anything approaching homely conditions ; five years later, the place was closed. West Sussex bought a country mansion in 1949 which was to provide a home for 70 children until 1954 ; its cottage homes, which had been opened in 1935 for 134 children, stayed in use until 1965. East Sussex opened five family group homes between 1953 and 1956 ; West Sussex opened two in 1954, although its children's officer had first suggested them four years earlier. (11)

If progress lurched, though, it can at least be said to have lurched with a fair sense of direction. The Home Office, in the early years of the service, was not just concerned with the where of care for children and the logistics of moving them from bad point A to better point B. It also issued a series of memoranda which had to do with the content of what was on offer.

A memorandum on residential nurseries in 1950 gives the tone : 'Regimentation and rigidity... are to be avoided at all costs. The wearing of overalls instead of uniforms and the avoidance of the use of nurse's headgear help towards a homelike atmosphere... While it is undesirable to force a child into independent behaviour too soon, it is equally undesirable to restrict his development by denying him the opportunity to do things for himself... It is important that children should hear the talk of adults and be talked to individually. Adult mental companionship is essential for development and the lack of it may lead to dullness and backwardness... Each child needs individual attention and interest if he is to form satisfactory emotional attachments to others... Mealtimes should be not only an occasion for social training but also for nursery staff to spend time with the children and to show them that they are cared for... Opportunities for walking, climbing and lively play are necessary to promote muscular development and these activities should be restricted as little as practicable.' (12)

In 1951, the Home Office issued a memorandum on the conduct of children's homes, which emphasised that the aim of new homes for those in long-term care was 'to enable each child to live as a member of a small group', and to enable children to mix easily with their school friends. The home, it said, would be more like a normal one if all spaces were common – with due respect for the privacy of staff and children. Each child should have a reasonable share in the running of the home – 'it is sometimes forgotten that [this] means a share in the interesting as well as in the dull occasions'. Children should be able to show their own taste in furnishing, colour schemes, clothes and personal possessions. Mealtimes were important and so was bedtime, when each child should be able to feel that he could talk to the housemother. 'The success of family life within a children's home will be seen to the degree to which a child who has been brought up there feels himself to be an individual with rights and responsibilities, equipped to take his place in the world. Every aspect of life within the home should contribute to this end, since the aim of all that is done is to produce stable, happy and self-reliant citizens.' (13)

25

By 1955, the Home Office was emphasising that 'the essential principle in any nursery, large or small, is that each child should have a member of staff to whom he can look for continuity of care' and a memorandum from its Advisory Council on Child Care was saying that nurseries with thirty places, as suggested in the 1950 memorandum, were too large to meet the children's need for individual attention. The Council emphasised the importance of trying to mitigate the effects of separation of the young child from the people he knew, especially his mother. Boarding out, it suggested, was preferable to a place in a nursery. (14)

This flow of guidance dried up once the children's departments were properly launched and the introduction of the new system in 1971 did not see anything like the same amount of central advice. In that year, the Department of Health and Social Security – which had taken over responsibility for children in care from the Home Office – brought out a design guide for community homes. This recognised that a community home is no complete substitute for the real thing, but emphasised that it should offer the children who live in it opportunities for a range of experience, from complete privacy to wider relationships within it and outside ; it was important to site these homes in urban areas with good public transport. The living groups should be of between eight and twelve children ; the entire unit could go up to fifty places if there was education on site. (15) Five years later, the DHSS produced a guide to foster care practice. (16) These are really its only two major pieces of advice since it became responsible for children in local authority care. The 1970s have mostly been taken up with debate about the workings of the 1969 Children and Young Persons Act and, later, the introduction of the 1975 Children Act – the second due partly to the considerable concern about non-accidental injury to children in their own homes.

There has, however, been continuing debate about the training of staff who work with children in residential care. The Curtis Committee, as we have seen, felt so strongly about the need for a training in child care in general that it produced an interim report on this. It was particularly concerned about training for residential care. In the past, it said, it had been thought that 'personal suitability and some domestic experience or handicraft' had been qualification enough ; but a full training was 'essential' if the general standards of child care were to rise. (17) The Central Training Council in Child Care which Curtis wanted was duly set up and there have been complaints about the shortage of trained staff ever since.

The Council offered a variety of training courses. By the end of 1960, the Home Office reported, 681 women and 67 men had a Certificate in Child Care, and 1772 of the first and 264 of the second a Certificate in the Residential Care of Children ; 5668 people had been on residential refresher courses. (18) In that year, 160 people received the Certificate in the Residential Care of Children ; this number rose steadily, to 275 in 1965. (19)

Yet at the end of the 1960s, only a third of the staff of children's homes had any formal training and only 18% a training in residential child care. Among senior staff, though, these proportions, by 1970, were far higher : over a half and about a third (20,21).

By 1974, it was reckoned that only 14% of staff in community homes had a training in residential child care, (22) but by then the whole question of what training should look like in the future was in the air. The Central Council for Education and Training in Social Work, which had taken over from the specialist training bodies when the generic social services departments were set up, proposed the abolition of any specialist training in residential social work, including that with children, in favour of a two-tier generic training pattern, leading either to a Certificate in Social Service or a Certificate of Qualification in Social Work. (23) The last intake for the specialist residential qualifications was in 1979/80.

By 1978, then, the specialist pattern of caring for children which the 1948 Act had set up had been merged into a general approach to social services. That specialist pattern, though, was a classic example of how a service can be built from scratch on a set of very clear principles. The next chapters look at how far that clarity of philosophy and action has been reflected in attitudes to and provision for other groups of children not living at home.

Notes

1 *Sixth Report on the Work of the Children's Department*, HMSO, 1951, para. 49.

2 *Report on the Work of the Children's Department 1961–3*, HMSO, 1964, para. 10.

3 *ibid.*, para. 14 ; *Report on the Work of the Children's Department 1964–6*, HMSO, 1967, para. 27.

4 *Sixth Report*, para. 56 ; *Seventh Report*, HMSO, 1955, para. 47.

5 Moss, P., 'Residential Care of Children, a general view', in Tizard, J., Sinclair, I. and Clarke, R., (eds), *Varieties of Residential Experience*, Routledge and Kegan Paul, 1975, p. 29.

6 *Sixth Report*, paras 61, 62.

7 *Sixth Report*, paras 64, 67, 69 ; *Seventh Report*, para. 53.

8 *Sixth Report*, para. 72.

9 *Our Large Family*, Lancashire County Council Children's Committee, 1955.

10 *The First Seven Years*, Cheshire County Council Children's Committee, 1954.

11 Jones, W., *The Development of Children's Departments in East and West Sussex*, MA Thesis, University of Sussex, 1975.

12 *Sixth Report*, pp. 122–26.

13 *Seventh Report*, pp. 104–16.

14 *Seventh Report*, pp. 117–20.

15 *Community Homes Design Guide*, DHSS Advisory Council on Child Care, HMSO, 1971.

16 *Guide to Fostering Practice*, DHSS Working Party on Fostering Practice, HMSO, 1976.

17 *Training in Child Care*, Cmnd. 6760, HMSO, 1946, para. 4.

18 *Report on the Work of the Children's Department*, 1961, paras 100, 106, 116.

19 *Report on the Work of the Children's Department*, 1964–6, para. 63.

20 National Institute for Social Work Training, *Caring for People*, Allen and Unwin, 1967, p. 113.

21 Moss, P, *op. cit.*, p. 42.

22 *Manpower and Training for the Social Services*, DHSS, 1976, p. 154.

23 Central Council for Education and Training in Social Work, *Residential Work is a part of Social Work*, 1974.

4 What place for handicapped children?

The Curtis Committee, as we have seen, had little to say about the needs of handicapped children in residential care. It accepted the existing arrangements with little criticism ; its greatest concern was that mentally handicapped children should be separated from normal ones. But in the nature of things, handicapped children have continued to come into care throughout the postwar period. So it is important, before looking at more specialist provision, to see whether the child care service felt able to bring them into its general provision, or whether it continued the policies of segregation that Curtis had recommended. On the whole, it opted for the second, and this pattern has been followed by social services departments. There have not been many signs either that these departments are putting much energy into developing overall plans for all the children for whom they are responsible – whether these are technically in their care or others who need residential provision. The regional planning committees set up under the 1969 Children and Young Persons Act by local authorities to plan for children's facilities deal only with children who are technically in care. Even though some of these children are bound to be handicapped, 'planning' for them has tended to consist of lists of available places tacked on to the original plans and their subsequent revisions. Most of the planning energy has gone into the much hotter political issue of community homes with education – the old approved schools. So throughout the period, the attitude of local authorities to handicapped children for whom they are responsible has been to find separate provision rather than to integrate them into existing or planned children's facilities.

And yet the numbers of handicapped children coming into care continued to rise. Although the total number is not available, the number in homes catering specifically for children with handicaps rose from some 1900 in 1951 to 2800 in 1976 (see Tables 3, 4). As early as 1952, one survey of children in local authority homes and nurseries turned up 565 out of a total of 13,154 (4.3%) who were handicapped in some way. By far the largest number of these were classed as 'educationally subnormal' : 365, or 2.8% of the total. Next came the 'mentally deficient' – 126, or 0.95%. There were 31 children with physical handicaps and 43 with both physical and mental handicaps – 0.23% in each case. (1)

By 1969, the Advisory Council on Child Care was looking at handicapped children in the care of eighteen authorities in London, precisely because it had been getting reports that their numbers were increasing ; children's officers, as well as being worried about the length of time these children spent in care, wanted to work out the implications for future staffing. In the eighteen authorities studied, it seemed that one in six children coming into care was handicapped. Even when the notoriously hard to pinpoint category of 'disturbed' children was left out, the proportion was still one in ten. (2)

Official attitudes to these children have veered from the strictly segregationist to cautious optimism about the possibility of bringing them into regular children's provision. The Home Office had made its own position on accepting mentally handicapped children into ordinary children's homes quite clear as early as 1938 : this was, it said, an 'improper practice'. Part of the problem at least seemed to be the very visibility of the handicapped children. 'At one preventive home for about 30 girls', said the Home Office, the acceptance of these children was 'a definite policy of the committee, and regarded as a social duty to the mentally defective who, it was maintained, were not noticeable : actually, the inspector had in a short visit noticed five out of the six'. (3) Nor was the Home Office, in the early post-war days, too encouraging about the presence of children with other handicaps in its homes ; 'such a child might be at a disadvantage or be a disturbing influence'. It did, however, feel that it was possible to board out backward or disabled children, even though some authorities thought this impracticable ; this could be envisaged for a child who needed special education, where a day place was available and a residential place was not. (4)

By 1955, the Home Office was reporting encouraging progress in the boarding out of 'special needs children' – which included those only in care for a short time, large families and those who needed holiday foster homes, as well as those with physical and mental handicaps ; fostering handicapped children was not easy, but it had found instances of this being done. (5) At the same time, it noted examples of severely handicapped children who were doing well in children's homes. One girl with cerebral palsy had been in a residential nursery until she went to a special residential school at the age of six : 'she has made extremely good progress and is a happy child'. Some voluntary homes were beginning to 'experiment' with the care of disabled children ; one girl without legs, for instance, was 'growing up happily' in one and going daily to the local school. (6) At least one authority, however, thought that the handicapped children in its care were better off out of its children's provision. In 1954, Somerset children's departments had 27 children in residential schools for mentally handicapped children (ESN schools) 5 in hostels for the maladjusted, the same number in a unit for psychotic children or mental institution, 6 in 'moral welfare' homes, 2 in voluntary homes, 8 in hostels for working boys, 2 in boarding schools, 1 (handicap, alas, unspecified) at a sea training school and 6 in private residential nurseries. (7)

In that year, the Advisory Council on Child Care issued a memorandum on handicapped children in the care of local authorities. (8) 'Some of these children,' it said, 'can be dealt with within the child care framework, given suitable facilities and adequate staffing ; others need special residential training, for example, in a boarding home for maladjusted children or in a boarding special school'. Where this could not be obtained immediately, local authorities were faced with a 'difficult task' in doing the best they could for the child.

The Council was not entirely pessimistic about the ability of the children's service to provide a home for handicapped children. Every effort, for instance, should be made to board out 'educationally subnormal' children, who usually did better in this setting than in a children's home. In homes, however, they 'seldom cause difficulty'; other children might develop a protective attitude towards them. Care was needed to ensure that the handicapped child didn't think intelligence was all that mattered : 'A child in his own home is loved and admired for many other things and it is important that a child in care should have the same satisfaction.' If there was no day special school in the area, the authority might have to set up a special home for this group of children near one ; in general, however, it was better for the handicapped child to be mixed with normal ones and there were additional disadvantages in having many children from homes in one school. If a special home was necessary, it should be well staffed, because these children needed more encouragement than others ; they quickly became isolated unless they had chances to meet other children.

For children with physical disabilities, by contrast, the Council advised a special home if they could not be boarded out – the scope for which was 'necessarily limited' ; there were, however, unlikely to be enough children to make this often possible. 'Maladjusted' children, though, should be segregated in a special home only as a last resort ; segregation brought the danger that they could be left there for too long. Diagnosis of 'maladjustment' was not easy and staff should be encouraged to give 'all possible help rather than to regard [the children] as necessarily in need of specialist treatment'. Even when the local education authority thought a child needed to go to a special school, a place might not be available ; in this case, numbers in any one home should be kept small and the staff ratio generous, with help from the child guidance and hospital services as necessary. Some local authorities had succeeded in boarding out children for whom special education was not thought necessary, by approaching 'selected sections of the community' ; if necessary, a higher rate should be paid to these foster parents. Finally, children's departments should provide for children certified as 'mentally defective' as best they could. The shortage of places in institutions was well known ; 'since it will seldom be practicable for a mentally defective child to be boarded out suitably, he must, unless placed in a voluntary or privately owned children's home with suitable facilities for such children, be accommodated in an ordinary children's home'. The Council did not minimise the 'serious problems' this could bring, with staff untrained to give the special help needed.

'Some mentally defective children, owing to their habits and delay or failure in establishing normal physical controls, are seriously disturbing to

31

other children and require constant attention if they are to be kept clean. A few are a danger to other children in the home and require constant supervision. The difficulty of protecting the other children from the defective child, and the child himself from the consequences of his irresponsible actions, cannot but be a cause of anxiety.'

The last thing to do was to establish a special home for these children.

'In the absence of expert supervision, the dangers of association of dangerous or uncontrollable children would be even greater where the other members of the group were slow and dull of intelligence. The staffing of a home with such a mixture of defective children would be a problem for any local authority. The provision of training and occupation by staff without special knowledge, even if they could be found to undertake it, would be of doubtful value. Moreover the duty of providing such homes rests on regional hospital boards and not on local authorities.'

Even though the Council saw children's homes as having a part to play in the care of only selected handicapped children, it did emphasise the importance of keeping contact with others who moved on to more specialised places. The local authority, for instance, should keep in close touch with children in its care in special boarding schools for the physically handicapped and maladjusted – by letters, parcels, and periodic visits. If at all possible, children in care should spend their holidays away from their boarding school, in either the same children's home or the same foster home each time. There should even be contact, perhaps, with mentally handicapped children in institutions, even though the children's department had handed over responsibility for them to the mental deficiency authority. (This transfer of responsibility for children in care was set out in Section 8 of the 1948 Children Act.) But 'since such a child in care may have no friend other than the children's officer or some representative of the children's services, it may be that, in some instances, local authorities... will want to keep in touch with him'.

Finally, the Council felt far more strongly about physically handicapped children in long-stay hospitals, some of whom had little contact with the local authorities in whose care they were. 'Other children have relatives to visit them and news of normal home activities, and children in care need the same... The more rigid regime of hospital life makes it particularly important that the child should have a background as nearly as possible like that provided by interested parents.' (8)

By 1961, the Home Office was sounding more cheerful about the possibilities of finding foster parents for handicapped children ; it was 'heartening', it said, to record how many people were willing to care for a child who was spastic or severely maladjusted, even though it was still difficult to find special residential provision for 'extreme cases'. (9) Two years later, a third of all the children boarded out in one area were said to be handicapped and there was even a cheering story of how an 'ineducable' boy, thanks to the care and encouragement of his house parents, had progressed to a training centre and was now working for the local authority, repairing council property. (10)

But in spite of these examples, the picture in North London at least was less optimistic than this by 1969. In its survey of eighteen authorities, the Advisory Council on Child Care reported that children were likely to stay longer than was thought good in nurseries or reception homes and that plans for their future were hampered for lack of resources. Shortage of provision for severely mentally handicapped children and severely disturbed adolescents led to 'second best solutions', which were unspecified but led to staff anxiety. Where there were good local special day schools, departments were trying to find children places in local homes or foster homes – answers which were 'obviously preferred' to sending children to special boarding schools. The preference for local provision meant that children's officers saw the need for more residential establishments in future, to meet a greater variety of needs – including units for severely handicapped children near day schools and training centres. (11)

The 1959 Mental Health Act had enabled local authorities to set up homes specifically for children with mental handicaps. But by the end of the first decade of the Act's life, they had hardly made much of this opportunity. Table 6 shows what progress was made.

Table 6

CHILDREN IN LOCAL AUTHORITY HOMES FOR THE MENTALLY HANDICAPPED, 1961–70

(MENTAL HEALTH ACT 1959)

England and Wales

1961	1962	1963	1964	1965	1966	1967	1968	1969*	1970*
145	225	362	587	689	995	1155	1341	945	1019

*England only

Sources :
Digest of Health Statistics, England and Wales, HMSO, 1969 Table 10.11
Annual Report, DHSS, 1970

The setting up of the new, comprehensive social services departments in 1971 in theory at least should have meant a closer integration of the care offered to handicapped children living away from home with that for the majority in local authority care. In particular, there was a new opportunity to integrate children defined as mentally handicapped into the general range of provision – whether they were technically 'in care' or not. As we have seen, the provision of homes for these children under the Mental Health Act passed from local health authorities to the new social services departments when these were set up.

Yet not much seems to have been made of this opportunity in the first years of the new social services departments. An enquiry by Campaign for the Mentally Handicapped in 1974 found that although a number of social services departments were occasionally integrating a few mentally handicapped children into their range of general provision, this was not a deliberate and thought-out policy. 'The opportunities presented since 1971 for exploring and developing the potential have', CMH concluded, 'been largely unexploited.' (12)

If social services departments have not done much to develop integrated services for this group of children, neither have they done much to develop specialist ones. Indeed, the slowness of these departments to offer mentally handicapped children a home has been one of the most disquieting features of the 1970s ; as the number of long-term hospital places has fallen (see Table 10), the shortfall in accommodation has simply not been taken up by social services provision and the conclusion must be that more families were caring for their handicapped child, with or without decent support services. In 1975, of the total of 7129 children discharged from mental handicap hospitals, only 26 went into local authority residential care. Three years later, the National Development Group, while pointing out that very many of these children had only been in hospital for a short stay from their family home, registered its 'great concern' at the low numbers going into local authority homes. (13)

By the mid-1970s, it was generally accepted that the number of places in these homes for mentally handicapped children had remained virtually unchanged since the new social services departments were set up. Exact figures, however, prove extremely difficult to track down. Table 7 gives the official tally, although the figures are incomplete and a change in the way returns were made in 1975 reduces their value still further ; the later figures are more accurate. What is interesting, however, is the increased reliance on private and voluntary homes, while the use of these for children in care has been falling steadily (see Tables 3, 4).

In short, then, whether handicapped children have come officially into care or whether local authorities have had a duty to find homes for them under the

Table 7

CHILDREN IN HOMES FOR THE MENTALLY HANDICAPPED, 1972-77

(MENTAL HEALTH ACT 1959)

England

	1972	1973	1974	1975	1976	1977
LA homes	1619	1756	1753	1285	1497	1619
Registered private and voluntary	NA	NA	NA	325	512	429

Sources :
DHSS statistics SSDA 107, SSDA 103
Homes and Hostels for the Mentally Ill and Mentally Handicapped, DHSS, 1977, a/f 77/11

Mental Health Act, there has been a reluctance either to integrate these children into regular provision or to set up specialist homes for them. This has meant a reliance on voluntary and private provision. It has also meant that many children have found themselves spending much – or indeed all – of their childhoods in institutions whose first focus is not on child care.

Notes

1 *Association of Children's Officers Bulletin No 16*, 1952.

2 Advisory Council on Child Care, *Handicapped Children in Care: an enquiry carried out by the London Region (North) of the Home Office Children's Department Inspectorate*, DHSS, 1971.

3 *Work of the Children's Branch. Fifth Report,* Home Office, HMSO, 1938, para. 108.

4 *Work of the Children's Department. Sixth Report,* Home Office, HMSO, 1951, paras 45–6.

5 *Seventh Report on the Work of the Children's Department,* HMSO, 1955, para. 33.

6 *ibid.,* para. 67.

7 *Report of the County Children's Officer,* Somerset County Council, 1954.

8 *Seventh Report on the Work of the Children's Department,* Appendix 5.

9 *Eighth Report on the Work of the Children's Department,* HMSO, 1961, para. 47.

10 *Report on the Work of the Children's Department, 1961–3,* HMSO, 1964, para. 16.

11 Advisory Council on Child Care, *Handicapped Children in Care,* DHSS, 1971.

12 Campaign for the Mentally Handicapped, *Integration or Segregation – the Choice in Practice,* 1974, p. 34.

13 *Helping Mentally Handicapped People in Hospital : a Report to the Secretary of State for Social Services by the National Development Group for the Mentally Handicapped,* DHSS, 1978, para. 3.1.8.

5 Children in special boarding schools

The number of special boarding schools has risen continually since the end of the war and so has the number of children in them. This has happened in the context of a rise in special education as a whole, and, in the early post-war years at least, of an enthusiasm for boarding education generally. In 1947, the Ministry of Education was reminding authorities that all children whose parents and local education authority (LEA) thought would benefit by it should go away to school instead of, as earlier, only certain handicapped children and others who could not go to day schools. (1) The hostels for 'difficult' children set up under the evacuation scheme had, it was felt, generally been a success and LEAs were encouraged to develop boarding homes attached to day schools as a variation on the boarding theme. As early as 1946, the Ministry of Education was asking LEAs to increase their boarding education for 'educationally subnormal' and maladjusted pupils, pointing out the advantages of country mansions. (2)

Although the enthusiasm for boarding schools in general may have waned during the last thirty years, they have remained an important part of the special education scene ; three out of five of the new places provided in the first decade after the war were, in fact, in boarding schools. (3) Both the Seebohm and the Warnock Committees wanted to see an expansion rather

Table 8

CHILDREN IN SPECIAL SCHOOLS, 1949–77

England and Wales, thousands

	1949	1951	1956	1961	1966	1971	1976	1977
Day schools*								
maintained	33.1	34.9	39.0	39.9	52.0	62.9	102.5	104.0
non-maintained				.1	.9	.9	1.0	.9
Boarding Schools								
maintained								
day pupils				1.5	2.3	4.4	7.8	8.1
boarding pupils				12.5	13.1	14.3	14.5	14.3
non-maintained	11.7	14.1	20.1					
day pupils				.4	.4	.8	.9	.9
boarding pupils				7.7	7.7	6.9	6.7	6.8

*includes hospital schools from 1966

Sources :
Annual Reports, Ministry of Education, HMSO, 1949, 1951, 1956
Statistics of Education, Vol.1, HMSO : 1961, Table 17 ; 1966, Table 35 ; 1971, Table 28 ; 1976, Table 23 ; 1977, Table 26

than a contraction of special boarding education. The first wanted an increase of boarding provision for maladjusted children in particular and a greater flexibility of this provision in general, with more hostels attached to day schools and more weekly and emergency boarding. (4) A decade later, in 1978, the Warnock Committee elaborated these themes. In addition to 'traditional' special boarding schools, it wanted others which offered a more flexible service. These should offer residential assessment ; they should offer opportunities to young people with disabilities to 'widen their horizons and increase their independence' during short stays ; they should offer intensive courses for pupils normally in day schools ; they should provide recreation and leisure facilities for children whose opportunities in special day schools were limited. Finally, they should take on a service which is traditionally completely outside the range of educational provision : they should offer short-stay facilities for children whose parents needed a break from looking after them at home. (5)

Table 8 shows how the provision of special boarding education has risen, in the context of a continuing rise in special education as a whole. (The large jump in children in special day schools between 1971 and 1976, however, reflects especially the fact that children hitherto classed as 'ineducable', including those in hospital mental handicap hospitals, were brought into the education system.)

In spite of the large increase in special school places, however, demand has continually outstripped supply, with waiting lists dominated by children defined as 'maladjusted' and 'educationally subnormal'. Table 9 gives an idea of waiting lists for both boarding and day places.

A second feature of post-war special education has been that as it has grown, so has it become more specialised. The 1945 regulations defined no less than eleven categories of 'special' children : the blind and the partially sighted, the deaf and the partially deaf, the delicate and the diabetic, the

Table 9

CHILDREN WAITING FOR PLACES IN SPECIAL SCHOOLS, 1949–77

England and Wales, thousands

	1949	1951	1956	1961	1966	1971	1976	1977
Aged 5+								
in day schools	NA		16.5	15.0	7.6	8.9	5.0	4.6
in boarding schools		20.1			5.1	4.5	2.7	2.0
Aged under 5								
in day schools	NA		.4	.3	.3	.5	1.4	1.2
in boarding schools					.2	.2	.2	.1

Sources :
Annual Reports, Ministry of Education, HMSO, 1949, 1951, 1956
Statistics of Education, Vol.1, HMSO : 1961, Table 20 ; 1966, Table 39 ; 1971, Table 32 ; 1976, Table 26 ; 1977, Table 29

educationally subnormal, the epileptic, the maladjusted, the physically handi-capped and those with speech defects. The early post-war years saw an enthusiasm for ever more specialised special schooling and new categories of school – and so of child – appeared within the official ones. A boarding school started for blind children with epilepsy, for instance, another for children with asthma, and the first for children with cerebral palsy began in 1947.

In 1953, diabetic children were classed with the 'delicate', which became a catch-all category for children not otherwise labelled, and the ten remaining categories were the statutory ones for the rest of the period. (6) But this didn't mean that specialisation stopped within them. Children defined as 'education-ally subnormal (severe)' joined the list when they were brought into the education system in 1970 ; the 1970 Chronically Sick and Disabled Persons Act provided for yet another category, the autistic, who started to appear separately in official returns.

None of this categorisation has been any guarantee that children end up in the schools best suited to their needs. In 1953, a report of the Ministry of Health Advisory Council for the Welfare of Handicapped Persons found that only a third of the children with cerebral palsy or epilepsy were getting the special schooling it reckoned they needed ; it pointed out that children 'unsuitable' for school – because of their low IQ or behaviour disorders – were taking places which others could use better, but they could not move out because there was nowhere else for them to go. (7) In 1968, the Seebohm Committee found 'children in approved schools who might have been better placed in special schools if their problems had been identified sooner ; children in special schools for the physically handicapped or the delicate who might have been placed in schools for the maladjusted'. (8)

A decade later, the whole system of classification on which post-war special schooling had been based was challenged by the Warnock Committee on special education. 'Categorisation', it said 'perpetuates the sharp distinction between two groups of children – the handicapped and the non-handicapped – and it is this distinction which we are determined, as far as possible, to eliminate.' It proposed the abolition of the statutory categories and new descriptive terms for children with difficulties in learning, in the context of its general approach that no less than one in five children in fact needed 'special education'. (9)

This, then, has been the general background against which special boarding education has developed. But the children in special boarding schools have not only been getting education. They have also been living away from their family homes for much of their childhood ; for some, their school has been the only 'home' they have known. We have seen how determined the Home Office was, particularly in the early post-war years, to ensure that children in care were, as far as possible, offered a real home. How far were the principles on which the developing pattern of child care was based reflected in official attitudes to special boarding schools ?

ASPECTS OF CHILD CARE

Aspects of child care

Certainly the rise in boarding education was not meant to be indiscriminate. The Chief Medical Officer of the Ministry of Education emphasised in 1953 : 'A child should never be removed from home unless it is quite certain that there is no practicable alternative. The security of the home cannot be lightly treated as a matter of no importance ; as a family unit, it is the fundamental basis for the child's emotional development and security ... A home is important to its children, even if it is a bad one.' He made a plea for keeping handicapped children in ordinary schools whenever possible. 'The reason for this is not a financial one, neither has it anything to do with administrative convenience ; it is made solely in the interests of the children themselves. They need an upbringing and environment as near normal as possible in order to help them to overcome their disability.' (10) Even earlier, he had taken on those social workers and teachers who had tried to persuade parents to send their children to the newly-opened boarding homes for diabetic children : 'Such attempts should be foiled. There is no substitute for a good home ; it is wrong to send to hostels children who can be looked after quite well at home.' (11)

In 1954, the Ministry of Education emphasised that no child should go to a special school unless he could not be educated in an ordinary one, and that where special education was necessary, a day school was preferable to a boarding one. (12) A year later, the Committee on Maladjusted Children emphasised the point : while children might have such disturbed relationships with their families that they had to leave home for a period, 'such treatment should be given only if it is clear that there is no hope of treating the child succesfully while he remains at home'. (13) And in the same year, Dr E. M. Bartlett, in a presidential address to the Special Schools Association, said that many members of the Association, largely because of John Bowlby's work on early maternal deprivation, were having second thoughts about residential schools. He hoped that the 1954 Ministerial advice stemmed from more than financial considerations : 'We are all, I think, coming more and more to realise that in trying to help a handicapped child we must keep clearly in mind that he is not so much a person with a handicap as a handicapped person and that whatever we plan for him must be planned for him as a person.' (14).

By the end of the decade, doubts about boarding schools had hardened further. The Chief Medical Officer spoke of 'a growing conviction that, with the best will and endeavour, a [boarding school] cannot reproduce the vital influences of childhood that only the home can give – those things that parents give naturally'. If boarding schools were essential,

'a small community and small groups in the dormitories, at meal times, when going out for walks and for other joint activities, are easier for children to accept ; to have their own possessions, their own clothing and pocket money, helps to strengthen their individuality which is threatened in community life and it is good if these things can be given by the parents.

39

Living in a boarding school may also mean separation from the ordinary life of the city and going to visit the shops or the cinema is apt to take the form of an expedition, instead of being an ordinary part of living.' (15)

Whatever the doubts about the wisdom of sending children to special boarding schools, however, the fact remains that these schools have been very much part of special education provision since the war ; indeed, as we have seen, if the Warnock Committee has its way, their role will be increased rather than diminished in future. What is remarkable, in view of this, is how very little official attention has been paid to the child care aspects of these schools. In spite of the fact that special education was officially seen as a 'welfare' service until 1964 – lumped in with school dinners and milk in every education annual report – it is only in the early post-war years that the fact that special boarding schools were a part-time home for their pupils seems to have exercised the official mind. Since then, the Department of Education has turned its attention to the quality of residential life in special boarding schools only once – and that only for children categorised as maladjusted. Although the Warnock Committee wanted special boarding schools to go far beyond an educational role, by providing short-term relief for parents, only four paragraphs in its very lengthy report can be said to have anything to do with the kind of life – as opposed to education – that children in boarding schools are offered.

The influence of the Curtis Committee's approach can be traced in some of the education reports of the early post-war years. In his annual report for 1946/7, the Chief Medical Officer (CMO) looked at the six boarding schools which catered for children with epilepsy. 'No part of a child's day', he said, 'is more important than that spent when the hours of formal instruction are over ; and it is that part of the child's daily life which the schools find difficulty in fully satisfying. Shortage of staff, especially of those experienced in the ways and needs of children, is at the root of the problems and anxiety experienced in some of the schools.' These could be considerable. In one school, the boys smashed every pane of glass and the bannisters as well – sheer boredom, the CMO reckoned. Whatever the shortage of staff, he found no excuse for them insisting, as they did in one school, that all children, including the fifteen-year-olds, went to bed at 6.30 pm even during the summer ; or for them forbidding the children to go out to play in case they met adult epileptics who lived in the same colony ; or for the fact that the last meal of the day was at 4 pm ; or for the lack of toys and recreational material. Each school, the CMO said, should introduce scouts and filmshows, sports and visits to shops. Parents' visits should be encouraged, all schools should have a good library and the censoring of letters should stop. Each child should have his own locker and his possessions must not be touched without his consent ; staff should remember that what looked like junk to them was 'often very dear to the heart of a boy'. (16)

In his 1950/1 report, the CMO carried an account by departmental medical officers of open air schools, to which 'nervous and highly strung' children were increasingly being sent. The inspectors were firm that most of these children should not go to boarding schools and neither should most 'delicate' children. 'There should be compelling reasons to justify the taking of a delicate child from the security of the warm and intimate affection of his family and placing him in a boarding school which is often austere and sometimes rigorous.' The schools, the inspectors found, were 'bare, cheerless and sometimes spartan'. Too few provided the curtains, rugs, pictures, individual lockers, bedside chairs and quiet rooms for older children which were 'not luxuries but necessities'. One school for 100 children had only one recreation room ; some dormitories had four or five rows of beds. In one school, there were no sheets on the beds but only rough brown blankets, even in summer. In another, the 'sick bay' consisted of three huts without running water or sanitation – the nurse had to wear wellingtons to get to it and, not suprisingly, no nurse ever lasted longer than three months. In yet another, the boys' urinals had been broken for a year and were hand flushed twice a week. In a few schools, meals had to be taken in silence ; children were sent to bed early and it was 'pretty obvious to them that bed is really being used as a means of getting them out of the way rather than to provide the rest necessary for their proper progress and development'. The inspectors saw no reason to increase the provision of open air schools. (17)

An alternative approach was outlined in a Department of Education and Science pamphlet on the education of maladjusted children in 1965. It was a rewarding exercise, it said, to compare home with school 'as objectively and imaginatively as possible'. It emphasised the importance of the 'small, comprehensible and intimate' character of home, of the child's sense of joint ownership and participation in it. 'Above all, he knows that he matters very much and that, come what may, even in spite of rows and punishment, there is someone who will always stand by him.' The report emphasised the importance of family groupings within the school, and said that although affection for the children could not be provided at will, many of its constituents could be : 'consideration, respect, individual attention, indulgence, sometimes even beyond the point of reason, praise for achievement, a surprise, a present, a treat, in fact anything and everything to convince the child that he matters for himself and not always as a member of a group'. (18)

Apart from these occasional concerns, there have been only two continuing debates which touch on the child care aspects of children in special boarding schools. The first of these has to do with the holiday arrangements made for children in care of local authorities who go to these schools. The second has to do with who looks after – as opposed to who teaches – them while they are at school.

As early as 1955, as we have seen, the Advisory Council on Child Care was urging that wherever possible children in care should spend their holidays from their boarding school in the same children's home or foster home each time. More than a decade later, a working party of the National Bureau for Co-operation in Child Care raised the same problem and underlined the importance of special education being provided in day schools for handicapped children in care. (19) The point was made yet again by the Seebohm Committee in 1968 : 'The total number of children is small, but it is indefensible that a child who is both handicapped and deprived of the care of his own parents should suffer further through the uncertainty of being sent to different foster homes or children's homes for successive school holidays.' (20) In spite of these exhortations, the problem remained. The Advisory Council on Child Care found, in its 1969 survey of handicapped children in the care of London boroughs, that children's officers were not keen to have these children in children's homes during holidays, because of crowding, changing staff, resentment from other children and staff anxiety. (21) In 1976, the Court Committee reiterated the plea that proper arrangements should be made for these children. (22) In 1978, the Warnock Committee urged social services departments to 'make every effort' to ensure that a stable home was provided for them, which 'so far as is possible' was the same for every holiday. It recognised, however, that there were some children for whom this arrangement could not work. Some children, it said, would have to return to hospital, as they did now, for the holidays : 'Where this is necessary, care should be taken to ensure that adequate staff are available and that stimulating activities are arranged for them.' An alternative would be to keep some schools open during the holidays. (23)

Staffing

Although there has, since the war, been an assumption that the staff of special boarding schools will include people other than teachers to help with the residential side of the children's life, there has been little determined recognition of the importance of child care skills in this setting. In 1952, the Ministry of Education notified education departments of three-week refresher courses for house staff. (24) But although the Committee on the Education of Maladjusted Children recommended three years later that training in child care should be given to everyone working as house staff in residential schools or boarding homes, it was not until 1959 that the training courses of the Central Training Council in Child Care were extended to them. (25,26) When a new in-service course was approved by the Council in 1967, the (by now) Department of Education hoped that this scheme would be used both for training new staff and for 'more systematic training for existing staff'. (27)

By 1970, however, only 9% of care staff in special boarding schools were trained residential child care workers. The attitude of the National Union of Teachers (NUT) to the care of children in these schools may have something to do with this low figure. In 1961, it had made its own position clear : it was teachers who were the most important child-carers in residential schools.

These teachers were, it said, a 'new profession', concerned as they were with the 'explicit teaching of the details of life' ; special boarding schools were by definition treatment centres and work in class was only of true value when supported by constant application outside. 'Teacher responsibility is the only answer', it concluded, and emphasised that 'welfare' staff must always be under teacher control. The NUT then stressed, and with no apparent sense of inconsistency, that teachers should under no circumstances be expected to take on more than fifteen hours extra duty a week. (28) A decade later, the NUT's views had not changed. 'In many cases, particularly in residential schools,' it said in its evidence to Warnock, 'teachers act as substitute parents.' But once more, it emphasised that they should not be expected to work 'excessive hours' and said that there was 'an urgent need for more supportive staff with adequate communication skills, in particular to supervise children outside class time'. (29)

The Warnock Committee did not entirely accept this view : both teachers *and* child care staff, it said, 'act in many ways as parents, and in special schools they are often seen as such by the children'. The contribution of child care staff was vital to the effectiveness of special boarding schools.

'Although child care work includes some domestic duties, these should not be so extensive as to limit the time which the staff can spend in personal contact with the pupils in the school. It should be recognised that child care staff have a responsibility for establishing close personal relationships with the children which supplement family experiences and that in many cases they may act as substitute parents. This is a facet of their work which has been adequately appreciated only in recent years and there is scope for its further development. Trained and experienced staff can create patterns of living which reduce the institutional effects of boarding schools and encourage individual development, and their independent contribution to children's development needs to be more fully recognised.'

The Committee recommended special training, leading to a recognised qualification, for child care staff in residential schools. It was not convinced that the proposed Certificate in Social Service would offer enough expertise in working with children with some disabilities. It also wanted to see the establishment of a deputy head post, to be responsible for all arrangements for residential care, which would be open to trained child care staff and so encourage and exchange of staff between education and social services departments. (30)

And there, at the end of 1978, the matter rested. A year earlier, *Special Education* had, in an editorial, summed up the position more plainly than Warnock did. It pointed out the difficulties of special boarding schools in attracting good care staff and berated the Central Council for Education and Training in Social Work for its failure to produce specific training proposals for this staff. It found that the Department of Education had been slow to give a lead and that residential care organisations had shown little interest. 'The hours outside the classroom are long,' it said, 'the living opportunities many – yet we persist in wasting so many chances to help children because of the failure of other professional staff concerned to acknowledge the importance of the child care teams.' (31)

So, in the two areas where the child care aspect of life in special boarding schools had been recognised at all, little had been achieved in the thirty years between 1948 and 1978. Children in the care of local authorities could still leave their special boarding school for holidays in either a bewildering succession of homes or even a hospital ward. The importance of the role of child care staff in their school lives was only belatedly being recognised. For the most part, the fact that these schools are home to the children who go to them for a good part of their year, and indeed of their childhood, had been virtually ignored in official guidance and statements. The whole elaborate structure of special education in boarding schools had developed with hardly any links with the system and philosophy of child care that grew from the recommendations of the Curtis Committee.

Notes

1 *Education in 1947*, Cmnd. 7426, HMSO, 1948, p. 52.

2 Circular 79, Ministry of Education, 1946.

3 *Special Educational Needs. Report of the Committee of Enquiry into the Education of Handicapped Children and Young People* (Warnock Report), Cmnd. 7212, HMSO, 1978 para. 2.49.

4 *Report of the Committee on Local Authority and Allied Personal Social Services* (Seebohm Report), Cmnd. 3703, HMSO, 1968, para. 241.

5 Warnock Report, paras 8.15–8.18.

6 Handicapped Pupils and School Health Service Regulations : SI 1945, No. 1076, HMSO ; School Health Service and Handicapped Pupils Regulations : SI 1953, No. 1156, HMSO ; Handicapped Pupils and Special Schools Regulations : SI 1959 No. 365, HMSO.

7 Circular 26/53, Ministry of Health, HMSO.

8 Seebohm Report, para. 174.

9 Warnock Report, chapter 3.

10 *The Health of the School Child : Report of the Chief Medical Officer of the Ministry of Education for 1952 and 1953*, HMSO, 1954, pp. 69, 77.

11 *The Health of the School Child : Report of the Chief Medical Officer of the Ministry of Education for 1948 and 1949*, HMSO, 1952, p. 64.

12 Circular 276, Ministry of Education, 1954.

13 *Report of the Committee on Maladjusted Children*, Ministry of Education, 1955, para. 239.

14 *Special Schools Journal*, vol. xxliv, no. 2, 1955.

15 *The Health of the School Child : Report of the Chief Medical Officer of the Ministry of Education for 1958 and 1959*, HMSO, 1961, pp. 117–8.

16 *The Health of the School Child : Report of the Chief Medical Officer of the Ministry of Education for 1946 and 1947*, HMSO, 1949, p. 87.

17 *The Health of the School Child : Report of the Chief Medical Officer of the Ministry of Education for 1950 and 1951*, HMSO, 1952, pp. 107–24.

18 *The Education of Maladjusted Children*, Education Pamphlet 47, Department of Education and Science, 1965, pp. 27–9.

19 Parfit, J. (ed.), *The Community's Children*, National Bureau for Co-operation in Child Care, 1967, pp. 80–1.

20 Seebohm Report, para. 243.

21 Advisory Council on Child Care, *Handicapped Children in Care*, DHSS, 1971.

22 *Fit for the Future. Report of the Committee on Child Health Services* (Court Report), Cmnd. 6684, HMSO, 1976, para. 16.18.

23 Warnock Report, para. 8.20.

24 AM12, Ministry of Education, 1952.

25 *Report of the Committee on Maladjusted Children*, Ministry of Education, HMSO, 1955, para. 466.

26 AM 6/60, Ministry of Education.

27 Circular 7/67, Department of Eduation.

28 *Conditions of Employment of Teachers in Residential Special Schools*, National Union of Teachers, 1971.

29 *Educating the Handicapped*, National Union of Teachers (no date).

30 Warnock Report, paras. 14.34–7.

31 *Special Education – Forward Trends*, vol. 4, no. 2, 1977, p. 7.

6 Children in hospital

The Curtis Committee had had little to say about the child care aspects of a child's life in hospital. It was left to one of its members, Dr J. C. Spence, Professor of Child Health at Durham University, to make the link between children living in children's homes and those living in hospital, and to see that while what was bad for one group was equally bad for another, the solutions for both could be the same. What he had to say about long-stay hospitals in 1947 remained the clearest statement of what was wrong with them and the best attempt to put it right for the next twenty years:

'A long-stay hospital can never be completely successful in providing the things of which a child is deprived, whatever the educational answer may be or however many their books, toys and cinemas. These may mitigate the deprivation but do not give the sense of personal attachment, the relationship, the companionship, which are necessary exercises for the mind of the growing child . . . The fault lies in the form and arrangement of most of these long-stay hospitals. They have been conceived too much as medical institutions and arranged too much as hospital wards. It would be better if the children lived in small groups under a housemother and from there went to their lessons in a school, to their treatment in a sick bay and to their entertainment in a central hall. There would be no disadvantage in the housemother having had a nursing training, but that in itself is not a qualification for the work she will do. Her duty is to live with her group of children and attempt to provide the things of which they have been deprived'. (1)

While Dr Spence's concern was with physically handicapped children, it was echoed, some twenty years on, for those with mental handicaps as well ; indeed, it was official concern with children in mental handicap hospitals that then spilled over to those in other long-stay institutions rather than the other way round. This section will look at the general context of official concern for children in hospital over the past thirty years ; then at the situation of, and official statements on, first physically and then mentally handicapped children in hospital, and finally at proposals which covered both groups.

Dr Spence had also turned his attention to the effects of hospital life on children who went in for only a short time. He described a typical ward routine and went on: 'This daily routine of anxiety, wonder, apprehension and sleep is better than it sounds, because it is made tolerable by the extraordinary resilience and gaiety of the children at every opportunity. Their cheerfulness keeps breaking through. But it is a deceptive cheerfulness.' He recommended the grouping of children's beds in units big enough to ensure the special training of staff, and the then revolutionary notion that each unit should have at least five rooms where mothers could live in with and care for and nurse their children under the supervision of staff. He himself had been practising this policy for all children under three for some years and had found nothing but advantages – to the child, the mother and the staff, 'who learn not only about the handling of a child but about life itself' as well as being freed to care for other children on the ward. (2)

When this lecture was published, it was the recommendation that mothers should be allowed to live in rather than the proposals for reforming long-stay wards which drew the attention of readers of the *British Medical Journal*. Children who went to hospital for a short stay have attracted a great deal of attention, in fact, over the whole of the last thirty years. Their emotional needs, their contact with their parents while in hospital and their separation from adults in properly staffed children's wards and units were recurrent themes throughout the period.

In 1949, the Ministry of Health issued the first of its circulars to hospitals on the need to lift restrictions on the visiting of children. It took the gingerly advice of its Central Health Services Council : 'under reasonable safeguards', children could be visited by parents or guardians 'with reasonable frequency and if necessary by appointment'. There seemed to be some subsequent confusion about what was reasonable, for in 1953, the Ministry was reporting that only 300 out of 1300 hospitals allowed children to be visited daily, the rest settling for weekly visits or, in the case of 150 of them, forbidding visits altogether. The Ministry urged daily visiting, as it did again in 1956, by which time the number of hospitals which allowed it had trebled and the number which allowed it not at all had fallen to 28. It might even be possible, the Ministry suggested at this point, to lift restrictions on visiting altogether ; this had been tried in Australia. (3)

This campaign got an influential boost in 1959, when the Central Health Services Council Committee on the Welfare of Children in Hospital (the Platt Committee) recommended that there should be no ban at all on visiting, subject to the ward sisters' discretion. It also picked up Dr Spence's practice of allowing mothers to live in hospital with their children, recommending that rooms should be provided for this. (4) The Ministry of Health backed the report and in 1966, having found that ward sisters were using their discretion to impose blanket restrictions on visiting, it told hospitals that in future only a consultant should have the power to restrict visiting, and then only for particular children on particular occasions. (5) By 1969, a survey of 203 hospitals showed that visiting was unrestricted or at the discretion of the ward sister in 60% of them. (6) Four years later, a survey of over 700 wards for children showed that only about a half allowed unrestricted visiting and that 8% limited visits to six hours during the day ; only two thirds of these wards offered overnight accommodation for parents. (7)

The Platt Committee had also been concerned about children in adult wards. It cited a study of four six-week periods, during which there had been

12,757 children in children's wards, but 2684 aged between one and eleven and 2382 aged between eleven and sixteen in adult wards. It recommended strongly that children should only be admitted to adult wards in an emergency, or if they needed highly specialised treatment. (8) By 1965, 5% of young children were in adult wards and another 15% in these wards, but screened off. The Ministry of Health asked hospitals to do something about it. Four years later, it again asked them to ensure that no child at all under the age of twelve would be admitted to an adult ward. In 1977, once more, it was asking health authorities to report on children not yet in paediatric departments and on their proposals to get them out of adult wards. (9)

Altogether, the Ministry (and later Department) of Health issued nine circulars on these issues between 1949 and 1977.

The issues were not, for most of the period, tackled in isolation, for the Platt Committee's recommendations had been set in the far wider framework of providing comprehensive paediatric departments, under the charge of specially-trained sisters and paediatricians. The Platt Committee had read the Curtis Report and was unanimous that the emotional needs of children in hospital should be considered.

'The Curtis Report dealt with, among other things, the difficulties arising in the lives of deprived children, and it emphasised the part played by unfamiliarity and separation. The child in hospital, particularly when separated completely from his parents, encounters conditions similar to those of the deprived child, with the added risk of painful and frightening experiences.'

A new approach to caring for children in hospital should be based on mutual understanding between parents and hospital staff, and an insight from the latter 'into the great advances in child care which have been made in the past 20 years or so'. (10)

In the context of its proposals for comprehensive paediatric departments, the Platt Committee made detailed recommendations on the design of children's wards. Children of the same age should be grouped together. Colour schemes and furnishings should be attractive and there should be a playroom which even children in bed could see into. There should be an abundance of good toys and even young children should have somewhere to store their own possessions. Part of each day should be set aside for play, with plenty of proper play material. Older children should be encouraged to have hobbies and might join scouts or guides. (11)

In spite of the plethora of official guidance, as we have seen, hospitals were slow even to separate all children from adults in their wards. By 1976, the Court Committee on Child Health Services concluded that we were still 'a long way from achieving' the comprehensive paediatric departments in general hospitals that Platt had recommended eighteen years earlier, even though these were 'central to the provision of a rational and humane district hospital service'. (12)

Nevertheless, for some twenty of the last thirty years at least there has been a recognition that hospitals must do more than treat children's illnesses, that they must take account of the emotional needs of children as well. How has this concern been translated for children who stay in hospital not for days or weeks, but for months and years – the children for whom hospital really does become a home, and may be the only one they have?

Children living in non-psychiatric hospitals

The Chief Medical Officer of the Ministry of Education was less than enthusiastic about Dr Spence's 1947 ideas. While it was true, he said, that Victorian hospitals tended not to lend themselves to modern ideas and had an institutional atmosphere, it was not practicable to set up small groups in all of them. In any case, there were some excellent hospitals for children. In two of the London County Council hospital schools, for 180 children with skin diseases and 480 children with eye diseases respectively, 'the professional care is of the highest, the education is really good and the children are happy'. A City of Manchester sanitorium for 200 children, some of whom spent years in bed, provided a youth club, scouts, picture shows ; it even allowed older girls, 'as a special privilege', to visit the domestic science centre in pairs for an hour or so in the afternoon to make themselves a cup of tea. 'The man or woman who does not feel a lifting of the heart after visiting such a hospital school . . . must indeed be sour of spirit.'

Nevertheless, the CMO did urge efforts to end the 'hospitalisation' of children – 'the children relying too much on the efforts of others and being too much cut off from the outside world'. He commended the hospitals which allowed children in wheelchairs to go to local shops : 'thus they preserve a sense of the value of money and they meet and mingle with their non-handicapped fellows'. (13)

'Hospitalisation' of children, in its more literal sense, has not yet ended, although the numbers who now live in hospital have fallen considerably since the war. It is perhaps a clear enough indication of how little attention these children have received over the years that exact numbers are impossible to find. Such figures as there are for non-psychiatric hospitals have to do with the number of children in hospital schools and it has been by no means sure over the years that all children in hospitals, whether their stay has been short or long, have received education. For what it's worth, in 1947 there were 95 hospital schools catering for nearly 9000 children – up to a third of whom, it was reckoned, stayed for less than three weeks. In the decade up to 1955, the number going to hospital schools was said to have fallen by 2000 – as the number of outside schools increased, particularly for physically handicapped children. (14)

The closest look we have yet had at children living for a long time in hospital came in 1969 – and even this was a survey of only some hospitals rather than a complete census. This survey found 1463 children in the sixty-nine hospitals studied who had been there for over four months ; just over a quarter had lived in hospital for eighteen months or more. Forty-nine of these hospitals had 20 or fewer children ; sixteen had between 21 and 50 ; two had between 51 and 75, one between 101 and 150 and one between 151 and 200. Eighteen of the hospitals were specifically for children, ten of them acute, while fifteen were orthopaedic hospitals, twelve general acute hospitals and twenty-four 'other'. 41% of the children were aged between five and nine, a third between ten and fourteen, 19% between two and five and 9% under a year (15). Although this information was nearly a decade old, it was still the most complete that the Court Committee on Child Health Services could come up with in its 1976 report.

These children, and others like them, have been cared for by nursing staff throughout the post-war period. Dr Spence's suggestion that children's wards should be run by house-parents seems to have been completely forgotten ; indeed, the emphasis has consistently been on getting properly-trained paediatric nurses to run them. The Platt Committee emphasised that a hospital ward was effectively a child's home for as long as he or she was there and stressed the importance of nurses and doctors learning to meet emotional as well as physical needs. (16) It recommended that the sister in charge of any ward or department where children were nursed should be specifically trained in the care of sick children. Eighteen years later, no less than 43% of them were without this training. (17) As well as the emphasis on getting properly-trained nursing staff, there has been periodic talk of the importance of play therapists for all children in hospitals. The Court Committee thought that in time play would be seen as part of the educational provision for children in hospitals, 'and financed accordingly'. (18)

The Platt Committee emphasised that its recommendations applied as much to children who spent long periods in hospital as to those who were only there for a short while. Although it made no special study of children in mental illness and mental handicap hospitals, it thought that its general approach was applicable to them too, and that some of its ideas could be taken up for them 'with advantage'. Children coming to non-psychiatric hospitals for a long stay, at least, should be carefully prepared and parents should have close contacts with staff ; mothers should be able to stay in the hospital with their child for the first couple of nights. It was particularly important that the children were occupied during the school holidays and that the hospital had a good library. If the child had no visitors, he might be given a 'foster family' close to the hospital. (19)

If the Platt Committee saw the problems of children living for a long period in hospital as fundamentally different from those in a ward for only a short stay, the Court Committee, in its 1976 report, paid even less specific attention to them : only three paragraphs in its lengthy report are devoted to their problems. But by then, the emphasis of concern had changed. While the Platt Committee made no specific study of children in mental handicap hospitals, but contented itself with pointing out that some of its ideas could be taken up for them 'with advantage', the Court Committee took the completely opposite tack : it had plenty to say on the long-term hospital care of mentally handicapped children and reckoned that some of its feelings about them applied 'with equal force' to children in non-psychiatric hospitals. (20)

Children living in mental handicap hospitals

The Curtis Committee found some 7500 children certified as 'mentally defective' in residential establishments approved to take them in. Many others were in mixed-age local authority mental deficiency institutions or approved public assistance institutions, some 300 in an assortment of homes. It was the 'unknown' number thrown into the mixed workhouse population which so appalled the Committee, and it was its recommendation that they should be removed to 'properly staffed Homes and Colonies' which set the tone of residential developments for them for the next decade and more. Admissions of children to the institutions – which were taken over by the National Health Service to become hospitals in 1948 – rose, and so did parental demand for places, against a chronic background of lengthy waiting lists, staff shortages and over-crowding.

The Mental Deficiency Acts, which until 1960 governed both children and adults ascertained as 'defective', envisaged no alternative to institutions for any mentally handicapped person who needed residential care. In that year, the Mental Health Act put into effect the recommendations of the Royal Commission on Mental Illness and Mental Deficiency which had reported three years earlier. Local health authorities were now also able to provide residential care – a responsibility which passed to the new social services departments in 1971. In spite of these changes, however, the hospitals have remained the major resource for the residential care of mentally handicapped children throughout this period.

The exact number of children in mental handicap hospitals is impossible to track for most of the post-war period – which in itself indicates how little

Table 10

CHILDREN LIVING IN MENTAL HANDICAP HOSPITALS, 1954–76

England and Wales

1954*	1958*	1963*	1969*	1971	1972	1973	1974	1975	1976
6982	8370	6997	6400	6419	6094	5671	5277	4933	3883

*Children aged 0–15 ; other figures, 0–16

Sources :
Annual Report, Ministry of Health, 1958
DHSS Statistical Report Series No.12, HMSO, 1971, Table 2
National Development Group, *Helping Mentally Handicapped People in Hospital*, DHSS, 1978, Table 1
DHSS Statistical Report Series No.22, HMSO, 1978, Table A.26.2

attention has been paid to them. It wasn't until 1952 that local authorities were asked to make separate returns on the children and adults with mental handicaps in their care. Published figures on the hospitals, however, did not make this distinction : children and adults were lumped together for many years after this. Table 10 gives such figures for children as are available.

Although the overall number of children living in mental handicap hospitals has fallen since the 1960s and particularly fast during the 1970s, reliance on these hospitals for short-term care has grown. This use of hospital places was introduced in 1952, when the service was faced with a waiting list of 4175 children, 2219 of them categorised as 'urgently' needing a place ; the Ministry of Health then suggested that children especially might be admitted to hospitals for periods of up to two months without being subjected to the lengthy formal admission procedures that were mandatory under the mental deficiency legislation. (21) Given the very slow growth of local authority places for children since the 1959 Mental Health Act (see Tables 6, 7), the pressure on hospitals to provide for children for short periods has not let up. Table 11 gives figures for admission of children to mental handicap hospitals.

As Table 11 shows, the number of very young children admitted to mental handicap hospitals has fallen considerably, particularly in recent years. But in the early post-war years, this was not so at all. Fountain Hospital, for instance, took in a tenth of all children admitted to hospital, and in 1953, 90% of them were under five and 20% under two ; the average age was two and a half. (22)

Policies and problems

In 1955, when the Advisory Council on Child Care was emphasising the serious effects of separating young children from the people they knew and suggesting that boarding out provided a better substitute home for the young child than a residential nursery, the Chief Medical Officer of the Ministry of

Table 11

CHILDREN ADMITTED TO MENTAL HANDICAP HOSPITALS BY AGE, 1954–76
England and Wales

AGE	1954	1966	1971	1972	1973	1974	1975	1976
0–2		76	104	102	84	59	89	83
2–5	1221	569	810	727	628	698	594	567
5–10		1100	2310	2123	2030	2221	2180	2312
10–15		822	2078	2075	2110	2202	2561	2770
TOTAL	1221	2567	5302	5027	4852	5180	5424	5732

Sources :
Royal Commission on Mental Illness and Mental Deficiency, 1957
Ministry of Health Statistical Report Series No.4, HMSO, 1969, Table 5
DHSS Statistical Report Series No.20, HMSO, 1977
DHSS Statistical Report Series No.22, HMSO, 1978, Table Al.2

Health was offering very different advice on the care of mentally handicapped children of the same age. 'If the child has emotional security and well-being', he said, 'and if it can be arranged for him to live at a level consistent with his powers, whether he be idiot, imbecile or feeble-minded, he may be happy in the community, at home or in an occupation centre ; or in a hospital. (23)

This view, however, was somewhat modified over the next couple of years. In 1956, the CMO was stressing that

'all young children . . . whatever their mental state, need love, security, companionship and stimulation if the personality is to develop normally . . . It may make all the difference to the future of a mentally defective child that the first few years of his life are spent either in his own or some other family home, where the household is not too complex and the members of it few and constant enough for him to know and establish relationship with them.'

Even a child in a mental deficiency hospital needed 'the care which a good mother would give'. But to provide this was by no means easy. It was impossible to ask a student nurse, who moved about the hospital, took her meals separately and had to work reasonable hours, to provide the same constant attention as a mother would. There were two solutions to this. Either the children in hospital were looked after by a nursing assistant 'who not being young and probably having children of her own is content to stay in one ward'.; or older mentally handicapped residents looked after the 'young and helpless patients'. 'The mental deficiency hospitals hold many pairs of friends who help each other, going about it may be hand in hand, or the elder holding the small one on her lap, and both so contented with the relationship that it would be a deprivation to both to break the care which one gives the other.' (24)

This idyllic picture, however, did not last. In 1957, the CMO had a different view of the needs of mentally handicapped children. They were, he said, 'by reason of their mental and emotional retardation . . . particularly dependent upon affection, individual handling and care. There can be no doubt that the inevitable deprivations associated with institutionalism bear particularly heavily on these immature children, so that many of them must function at a lower level, physically, mentally and emotionally, as a results of removal from home. (25)

Children who were admitted to mental deficiency institutions had to be certified as 'defective' if they were to remain there for longer than the short-term visit allowed from 1952 on. As so many were admitted so young, it is not surprising that not all of them turned out to be 'mentally defective' at all. Fountain Hospital, for instance, had forty-one 'ineducable' children transferred to education authorities between 1949 and 1954. (26) The National Spastics Society told the Royal Commission on Mental Illness and Mental Deficiency of one hospital where there were some 300 spastics, a quarter of them children ; 'Only about a third of them are really certifiable, the rest are in need of institutional care.' (27) A year earlier, the Ministry of Health Advisory Council for the Welfare of Handicapped Persons had acknowledged that some children with cerebral palsy, dubbed 'imbecile', were in fact 'unable to express themselves and suffer great distress'. Others, however, 'take great pride in doing jobs of work to help their fellow patients and . . . appear to be quite content'. It hoped, nevertheless, that if children with cerebral palsy were found to be intelligent, special units could be set up which would help them develop so that they could perhaps move to a special school. (28)

The British Psychological Society, in its evidence to the Royal Commission, underlined the damaging effects of mixing people with different abilities, especially children.

'The idiot, the imbecile and the feeble-minded child (sometimes of potential normality) may play together ; the epileptic, the deaf and dumb, the spastic and the near psychotic are cared for by a changing staff inadequate in number and often in quality. Inevitably, under such conditions, individual progress may be adversely affected. (29)

While it had to tackle this sort of evidence about the current state of the specialist institutions, the Royal Commission had also to take on board the resistance of some local authorities to any increase in their own responsibility for mentally disordered children within their ordinary children's services. Dr J. A. Scott, for instance, Medical Officer of Health for London County Council, gave firm evidence to the Commission :

'If the children's committee could have taken action successfully [under the children's legislation], which is doubtful, they would immediately have raised a tremendous problem for themselves by taking a child who is not by definition an ordinary child and mixing it with other children, and they already have considerable trouble with the mental children [sic] who do come their way and of whom we have to take steps to relieve them. It would have been an unfair burden on the children's committee, or the children's officer, to have to take this case and even more unfair on the children with whom this child would mix.' (30)

The Royal Commission, which reported in 1957, took a cautious line on the future responsibility for mentally handicapped children. 'The attitude to the children and their parents . . . should certainly be more like that in the other child care and education services', it said. But it rejected a suggestion that these children should come out of special legislation altogether, with the protection of ordinary children's legislation instead ; it felt that they might need more than this – and so they were to continue to be classed with mentally handicapped adults. (*329–30*)*

This segregation of mentally handicapped children from others was also

*Numbers in italic in brackets refer to paragraphs in the Royal Commission's Report, Cmnd. 169.

written into the Commission's recommendations about the future responsibility for residential care for them and for disturbed children as well.

'Most of these children need specialised care of a type which would more suitably be provided through the mental health services than through the child care services, though in this, as in other respects, there should be co-operation and flexibility between the various local authority and hospital services. Neither the law nor administrative practice should rigourously exclude subnormal children from the child care services if they can suitably mix with other children.' (651)

In general, the Commission thought that children who could go to ordinary or special day schools (ie, those not excluded from education because of the severity of their handicap) were suitable for ordinary children's homes or foster homes ; others might need special boarding schools for the maladjusted or educationally subnormal. Children who were 'unable to benefit even from these special forms of education' might be 'successfully brought up by the local authorities', either under the children's department or under the mental health department, according to the way each authority wanted to organise itself.

'But although local authorities should be free to undertake the residential care and training of such children, we think it probable that the majority of the severely subnormal children who require training rather than education and also need residential care will be found to need special care for a period at any rate under psychiatric supervision in hospital.' (652)

The Commission did, however, make one further recommendation about the involvement of children's departments with mentally handicapped children. If a child in care went to hospital, the authority should have a positive duty to act towards it as a good parent, without interfering with the work of the hospital, and any bar to this should be removed. (653) This recommendation was enshrined in the 1959 Mental Health Act. (31)

The introduction of the Act found the Ministry of Health in considerable uncertainty about the future need for hospital places for mentally handicapped people, both children and adults – while it was 'clear beyond any reasonable doubt' that places for people with mental illness would halve over fifteen years. Demand for mental handicap hospital places was continuing to rise, almost entirely for 'low-grade' patients. In the very long run, the Ministry surmised, the hospitals might cater only for the people whose physical and mental handicaps were such that they could not be managed in the community, and for those whose emotional instability meant that they needed treatment under psychiatric supervision (32). This was the start of a debate about exactly who the mental handicap hospitals should be catering for that has continued ever since – and with only elaborations on this introductory theme.

Meanwhile, the hospitals were there, and in 1965 the Ministry issued its first guidance on 'improving the effectiveness of the hospital service for the mentally subnormal'. This tried to take further the question of whom the hospitals should really be serving by identifying seven categories of patient : those who require constant nursing care, special methods of diagnosis, or hospital treatment but 'cannot be admitted' to any other NHS hospital because of their behaviour or degree of handicap ; those with marked physical disabilities who cannot be cared for at home, or whose behaviour is too disturbed to be contained in the community, or who need treatment or training in secure conditions; and those who normally live at home but need short-term care. No distinction between children and adults was made in this list, although it was suggested that children with physical disabilities might more often be suitably cared for in paediatric units.

The aim of the hospital, the Ministry said, should be to develop the maximum social independence of each patient ; there should be the least regimentation possible and individual initiative among patients should be encouraged. No ward should normally cater for more than twenty children and they, like adults, should have their own clothing. Mentally handicapped children 'need the same sort of stimulus and sensory training as normal children obtain from play, exploration and affectionate care. Many of their problems can be met by modern methods of child care and rearing. Paediatricians, psychologists, nursery nurses, nursery school teachers and others used to dealing with normal children can usefully advise.' Each child needed his own possessions and toys and there should also be a large stock of playthings for the ward. Finally, children under five should be reviewed to see if they could go to an ordinary school. (33)

This last attempt to sort out the medley of children who had found themselves in mental handicap hospitals echoed a memorandum on the development of units for mentally ill and seriously maladjusted children and adolescents, issued a year earlier. This set out targets for provision and said that where units should be depended on local circumstances ; existing accommodation at or near psychiatric hospitals, paediatric hospitals or paediatric departments were among the alternatives suggested. Some long-term beds could be provided at mental subnormality hospitals for children 'who function at the subnormal or severely subnormal level', but there should be co-operation between specialists in mental handicap and child psychiatrists to ensure that 'a sufficiently stimulating' environment could be given. (34) One other attempt to sort out the children was launched by the Department of Education in 1968, when it asked LEAs to identify children now in mental handicap hospitals who would be 'equally well or better placed in residential schools or hostels provided or used by local education authorities *if a sufficient number of suitable places were available*'[their italics]. (35)

The debate about the role of the hospitals continued throughout the decade. By 1969, the Chief Medical Officer was reporting that while one school of thought claimed there need be no hospital beds at all for mentally handicapped people, another was saying that these beds should be in general hospitals and that children should come under the care of the paediatrician. The Ministry was saying, as it had said for some time, that no new mental handicap hospitals should have more than 500 beds. There was, thought the CMO, 'clearly room for wide experimentation and evaluation'. (36)

In the event, the evaluation came dramatically and in a form which made it clear that something more than a general exhortation to 'wide experimentation' was urgently needed. The report of the Committee of Enquiry into conditions in and events at Ely Hospital in Cardiff, published in 1969, revealed not only appalling conditions in that hospital but a serious failure of management. (37) The publication of the report and the disquiet it aroused led to three major initiatives : the setting up of the Hospital Advisory Service to visit and report to the Minister on long-stay hospitals ; the introduction of a programme of minimum standards to be met by the mental handicap hospitals ; and a policy working group whose work was eventually to be incorporated into *Better Services for the Mentally Handicapped.*

This White Paper, published in 1971, set out targets for the overall development of hospital and community services to mentally handicapped children and adults over a twenty-year period. It rehearsed the short-comings of existing provision – finding local authority services to be 'grossly deficient' in quantity and 'falling rather than rising' standards in the hospitals. It set out fifteen general principles on which 'current thinking' about mental handicap was based. Among these:

– a family with a handicapped member has the same needs for general social services as all other families ;
– mentally handicapped children and adults should not be segregated unnecessarily from other people of similar age, nor from the general life of the local community ;
– each handicapped person should live with his own family as long as this does not impose an undue burden on them or him, and links with the family should normally be maintained when he leaves home ;
– the range of services in every area should be such that the family can be sure that their handicapped member will be properly cared for when it becomes necessary for him to leave the family home ;
– any substitute home, whether temporary or permanent, should be 'as homely as possible, even if it is also a hospital. It should provide sympathetic and constant human relationships' ;
– there should be close collaboration between social services departments and other services – for instance, child health services and education. (38)

Residential accommodation was, the White Paper said, a local authority responsibility ; hospitals would in future provide treatment, not residential care. For children, this care could be with foster parents, or in an ordinary or specialist children's home. Any residential establishment should be 'homely', with a maximum of twenty places, and with access to local shops, parks and so on. While links with the family should be maintained, 'a new lasting relationship should be formed with the people in the new substitute home'. (39)

Hospitals, however, were effectively homes as well as places of treatment, and these should be governed by the same principles as homes in the community.

'The conditions and general atmosphere should be as homelike as possible, with every appropriate stimulation through education, industrial or occupational therapy and leisure activities and personal possessions for every patient. If staff are allocated to care for small groups of patients, individual attention can more easily be given and personal relationships be established.'

Contact with families should again be maintained, which meant that hospitals should be accessible to the populations they served. (40)

To put these principles into action, the White Paper proposed a twenty-year plan to halve the number of adults living in hospital and to reduce the number of children living in them from 7400 to 6400, with a corresponding increase in local authority residential and day services ; this, it felt, would ensure that only those who needed 'treatment' would in future be catered for in hospital. At the same time, there should be an increase in 'hospital treatment for day patients' – provision for adults with severe physical handicap or behaviour disorders should be increased from an estimated 500 places to 4900, and for children with the same degrees of handicap from an estimated 200 to 2900. (41) It was premature, the Government said, to decide a final future pattern for hospital services : 'alternative lines of development' should be encouraged, including the retention of hospitals of over 500 places (although not their expansion), the building of new hospitals of up to 200 places and smaller dispersed units. New facilities for children would normally be separated from those for adults, having close links with the children's department in the local general hospital and being organised in small, domestic units. (42)

This plethora of choice had been further spelled out in DHSS guidance a couple of months *before* the publication of the White Paper. Long-stay hospital places for mentally handicapped children, the DHSS said then, should be in 'special domestic type units on the general hospital site or in the children's units of special hospitals for the mentally handicapped or in special units on hospital sites or in the community associated with such hospitals'. Children with chronic physical illness or handicap should preferably be cared for in 'domestic-type units rather than conventional wards', but on the general hospital site. (43)

The White Paper recommendations for the future of residential services for mentally handicapped children were made in a general context of recommendations for *all* mentally handicapped people, whether adults or children. The 1976 report of the Court Committee on child health added a further dimension to the debate by setting its proposals for mentally handicapped children firmly in the context of recommendations for a child health service for all *children*.

This Committee was emphatic that 'chronic illness, handicap and psychiatric disorders are now at the centre of paediatric care'. It was equally clear about its objectives :

> 'we want to see a child and family-centred service, in which skilled help is readily available and accessible ; which is integrated in as much as it sees the child as a whole, and as a continuously developing person. We want to see a service which ensures that this paediatric skill and knowledge are applied in the care of every child, whatever his age or disability, and wherever he lives, and we want a service which is increasingly oriented to prevention.' (44)

The Committee wanted children to be treated at home rather than in hospital whenever possible, with paediatric general practitioners and child health visitors to provide primary care for them. A district handicap team would care for all handicapped children, working from the district general hospital. Support services for mentally handicapped children, as for others with handicaps, would be provided by paediatricians and child psychiatrists. These support services

> 'should no longer be so sharply differentiated from those for more intelligent children, nor should they remain so predominantly the professional responsibility of specialists in mental subnormality. These specialists are psychiatrists and they need to be freed of their other responsibilities to enable them to provide the psychiatric services which are in such short supply.' (45)

The Committee reckoned that three-fifths of the children living in mental handicap hospitals could have been placed in local authority homes if these had been available. Overall, it estimated that there should be residential accommodation for a third of all severely mentally handicapped children ; although it did not feel able to divide this responsibility out between hospital and local authority, it reckoned that at least half the places should be provided by the latter. For their provision, it hoped, hospital authorities would pick units attached to general hospitals rather than another of the DHSS options ; these units should be part of the children's department, but near the hospital rather than within it, to improve the children's prospects of integration into the community. Its recommendations for short-term care added further options to those already on the table. This could be provided jointly by health and local authorities; there should be ten places in each health district for the short-term care and treatment of mentally handicapped children with psychiatric disorders ; and there was room for 'experimental centres for handicapped children', which would act as a focal point for all services, including short-term residential care. (46)

The National Development Group, set up in 1974 to advise the Secretary of State on the development of mental handicap policy, agreed with the Court Committee that 'severely mentally handicapped children have more in common with other children because of their childhood than they do with severely mentally handicapped adults because of their common disability'. It even added an italicised rider: *'These children are children first and handicapped second.'* But its conclusions were different from Court's. While that Committee had envisaged the integration of handicapped children under a district handicap team and much closer integration through this with other child health services, the National Development Group saw a perpetuation of separate services to mentally handicapped children, bracketed still with mentally handicapped adults. Its proposed community mental handicap team, dealing with children and probably adults as well, was a 'high priority'. This would act as 'a kind of local task force, as a source of advice and support both for the mentally handicapped and their families and for other staff who come into contact with them . . . as a catalyst to the development of local facilities and resources and to the participation of the local community in working with mentally handicapped people'. (47)

At the beginning of 1978, the Government accepted the 'overall philosophy' of the Court Report – although it threw out the proposals for specialist paediatric general practitioners and health visitors, and made clear that each health authority should go about the integration of child health services in its own way. The principle of the district handicap team was accepted: this should provide 'a framework within which *all the needs* of the relatively few children with severe handicaps, both physical (including sensory) and mental can be met' [my italics]. But the National Development Group's idea of a community mental handicap team also found favour; referrals could be made to it 'where the District Handicap Team, for a variety of reasons, *may not be able to provide the help required'* [my italics]. (48)

So by the end of the period, the framework within which residential services to severely mentally handicapped children would be provided in future was far from clear. So, indeed, was the shape of those services themselves. Although, as Table 10 shows (page 51), the number of children in mental handicap hospitals was already far below its 1991 target by the mid-1970s, there was no revision of this target or official clarification of the multiple-choice alternatives to mental handicap hospital care.

The National Development Group had, however, defined 'perhaps the most important single target' – a review of the needs of each child in hospital to ensure that he or she was in the most appropriate setting. It proposed three main goals which touch on residential care. 'No mentally handicapped child should ever be admitted to hospital unless all concerned agree on the nature and degree of the disability which renders him unable to live in a community setting and unless his condition continues to require direct access to the specialist service *actually available in that hospital* [its italics].'

Children who no longer needed full-time residential care in hospital should be 'relocated' in their own families if possible, or in the community, without delay. And finally, all children had the right to a home run on domestic lines, supported by the NHS when multiple handicaps or disturbance of behaviour became too much for a domestic setting to handle. (49)

These goals were officially accepted at the end of 1977, when the Secretary of State for Social Services endorsed the need to end admissions of children to hospital for the 'wrong reasons' and to review the needs of those already there. (50) By the next summer, a draft circular asking local and health authorities to agree a date by which 'inappropriate' admissions would end was being discussed. But debate on what constituted an 'appropriate' admission under this rubric still continued.

It was left to the Jay Committee on mental handicap nursing and care, in its 1979 report, to push this debate a stage further. It noted that the main alternative for children to living with their families remained, in fact, a mental handicap hospital. 'We find this,' the Committee said, 'quite unacceptable'. Its proposed model of care was firmly based on the principle that *all* mentally handicapped people, whatever their ability or disability, have a right to enjoy normal patterns of life within their community. Mentally handicapped children should be able to live with a family. 'The first question to be asked must always be "How can we provide support which will allow the child to continue to live with his own parents and his own brothers and sisters, in his own home, in his own community ?" If this proves impossible, we must look first to a long term placement with a substitute family.' A second alternative would be a place in a children's home in which children without handicaps also lived, while the needs of a small number of mentally handicapped children would best be met in specialised homes. Whatever the accommodation, however, it should be local to the child's own family, which would remain closely involved in his care. The living group should be small – of between four and six children.

'The small unit which we envisage is a place where residents and staff live together as a unit, a place where meals are cooked, washing-up is done and tradesmen are seen. In such small homes, whether general or special, the child will experience as normal a life as possible and he will be cared for by staff, both men and women, trained in the care of children living separately from their parents.' (51)

Finally, the Committee debated the merits and drawbacks of highly specialised units, provided on a regional basis for a small minority of children and adults with profound or multiple handicaps and very severe disorders of behaviour. It concluded that although there was room for this sort of accommodation within its model of care, the onus was on its supporters to demonstrate its value. It should, in any case, be seen as offering clearly defined treatment rather than residential care, and people would leave it for their own home as soon as possible. If specialist units were set up, they should wherever possible share the characteristics of local homes. There was little merit, and considerable disadvantage, in clustering a number of specialist units on one site. (52) The Jay Committee, in short, saw no future at all for the mental handicap hospital as we know it.

The Committee's model of care was still under discussion at the end of the period. So were its recommendations on another essential element in the residential care of mentally handicapped children : the training of those who look after them.

Staffing

Throughout the post-war period, staff who look after children in mental handicap hospitals have not been expected to have a training in child care, or even in paediatric nursing. They have been expected to be trained in the care of mentally handicapped children and adults as a group. In 1976, some 10,000 of the staff working in mental handicap hospitals had this training, while some 9000 were nursing assistants with either minimal training or none at all and another 3000 or so were being trained. (53)

In 1967, the Royal College of Nursing stated firmly: 'It is the function of nurses in hospitals for the mentally subnormal to meet the physical, educational and social needs of patients' – which included 'feeding', hygiene, training children on the ward and in school and training adults for employment. It saw the ward as the centre of operations : the 'school habit' and the 'work habit' were to be formed there. It regretted that others were increasingly invading nursing territory. 'It is a tragedy that in so many hospitals children and adults have been trained from admission by the nursing staff in the ward and then from 9.30 am to 4.30 pm are handed over to other people for similar training. In far too many situations this has led to a lack of co-operation between the ward, the hospital school and other departments, to the detriment of the patients.'(54) This lack of co-operation can still go on, in spite of official recognition that mentally handicapped children, no less than others, have the right to be taught by a teacher in a properly constituted school.

The current training syllabus for mental handicap nurses, published in 1970, reiterates that the nurse should be 'fully conversant with all aspects of the care, education and training of the mentally handicapped in hospital and in the community'. The course covers child development in a section devoted to human growth and social relationships. As Campaign for the Mentally Handicapped has pointed out, however,

'whatever the formal context of the syllabus, one only has to talk to student and pupil nurses to find out where the informal emphasis is laid. Too often, nurses in training come to see the social aspects of care as 'frills on the cake' – the minority-time subject, rather than the core of the work. The structure of the examinations, moreover, enables them to pass with merely a casual awareness of these aspects.' (55)

At the beginning of the 1970s, questions began to be asked about whether nurses should care for mentally handicapped people at all. The Briggs Committee on Nursing thought that in due course a new 'caring profession', divorced from nursing, should probably evolve ; it also thought, however, that a paediatric nurse with experience in both a sick children's and a mental handicap hospital would be 'uniquely well prepared to care for the child handicapped in both mind and body.' (56)

The Court Committee disagreed with this proposal for a new 'caring profession', pointing out that there were some children for whom predominantly nursing care was 'indispensable'. Children who did not need nursing should not be in hospital. If they did have to remain there, wards should be radically reorganised into 'homes', staffed by child care staff with visiting nurses and doctors. (57)

The Jay Committee's proposals for the training of staff of residential homes, for both adults and children, were the logical outcome of its philosophy and model of care. It proposed a common training for staff working in health and social services establishments to replace current nursing and social work qualifications. The majority of the Committee recommended that this training should be the responsibility of the Central Council for Education and Training in Social Work (CCETSW) and that the qualification offered should be the Certificate in Social Service (CSS). Staff who wanted to work with children would take a specialist training unit within the common framework of the course, leading to a Certificate in Social Service (Mentally Handicapped Children). In addition, the Committee recommended that CCETSW and the General Nursing Council should together develop post-qualifying courses for general, psychiatric and sick children's nurses, and residential care staff working with very severely handicapped people. Overall, the Committee wanted to see a doubling of the present numbers of residential staff, half of whom would hold the CSS. Basic care staff would receive at least two weeks' in-service training each year in the fundamental principles of residential care. (58)

If these recommendations are accepted, mentally handicapped children will, for the first time, be cared for by people who are trained child care workers as well as having a specialist understanding of their handicap. The residential care of mentally handicapped children will at last become part of the general pattern of child care in this country.

Concern for quality

It was not until 1972 that the Department of Health and Social Security issued any guidance which touched specifically on the quality of the life children led in long-stay hospitals – whether their handicaps were physical or mental.

In that year, it put out suggestions on maintaining family links for all children in long-term hospital care. Unrestricted visiting should be encouraged, it said; overnight accommodation for parents at the hospital and regular home visits for the child were helpful. The responsible consultant should make a point of seeing parents when a child was admitted and social workers should be in touch with the family. Where contact with parents looked like being lost, or actually was, there should be liaison between hospital and local authority.

Hospitals were reminded that although they were not empowered to assume parental rights if a child was 'abandoned', local authorities were. Less administratively, each hospital authority should 'seek to provide as full and as happy a life as possible for children while they are in hospital. In particular, staff should seek to ensure that the child who has lost contact with his parents has the secure and emotionally satisfying relationship which is essential for normal development.' The potential of volunteers to help provide this relationship was stressed. (59)

Hospitals varied in the enthusiasm with which they responded. A year later, while some mental handicap hospitals had immediately informed local authorities of 'abandoned' children, others had not. The Hospital Advisory Service, which had been set up to visit long-stay hospitals in 1969, seized the essential point. 'None, indeed, looked to the deeper implications that hospital children (including multiply-handicapped long-stay children) can live in conditions which fall far short of the standards of child care expected in other residential accommodation.' (60) It was the clearest official recognition yet of how far standards between groups of children living away from their own homes had diverged over the past twenty-five years.

In 1974, the DHSS issued a paper on 'the quality of life' for long-stay children in hospital, based on a conference it had held on the subject. It tried to tackle the 'common factor of crucial importance' to all these children : that hospital had to serve as home, either temporarily or permanently. It pointed to the accumulated weight of evidence on the adverse affects of deprivation of normal family life on a child's physical, emotional and intellectual development, and emphasised the importance of understanding the 'total parental role and the apparent uniqueness of the individual family and the bonds between a particular child and its parents'. It pointed out that however good the links of the child with his natural family, much parenting would fall to the nurses with whom the children were in contact. It found 'patient assignment', which could allow the child to relate permanently to a small number of adults, 'an undoubted step forward'. 'This staffing pattern may be demanding of resources and need to be attained gradually, but it can well be argued that the children's well-being is the overriding consideration and the problem becomes a question of priorities of expenditure.' Whether this pattern was developed by individual hospitals or not, psychologists and psychiatrists could help develop in-service training to give staff and voluntary workers insight into children's social, emotional and intellectual needs.

The paper also looked at how children in hospital could have experience of domestic life. Some cooking, washing-up, washing of clothes and other domestic tasks could be encouraged, although these 'clearly would not replace the hospital's centrally organised services'. The children should, 'as far as possible', have the same daily routine as in a normal home. Staff should wear ordinary clothes rather than uniforms ; children should have their own possessions and a place to keep them ; ample play material should be on hand and there should be contact with the outside community. (61)

With this paper, the DHSS was finally tackling for children in hospital some of the problems which had been tackled for children in the care of local authorities over two decades earlier – and coming up with much the same suggestions for alleviating them as the Home Office had then. The Court Committee liked this paper so much that it recommended, in italic print, that it should be more widely distributed. (62) Two years later, in 1978, the National Development Group also emphasised how much good advice there was in this paper. But, it added, 'in many areas the circular seems to have sunk without trace in the maelstrom of NHS reorganisation'. (63)

As the period closed, however, there was a growing recognition – for mentally handicapped children at least – that the present hospital service was incapable of meeting their needs. More than thirty years after the Curtis Committee reported, the National Development Group took up part of its unfinished business with more determination than had yet been officially seen.

'We must state categorically that the large mental handicap hospital can never provide a satisfactory substitute home for any child. No one now questions the vital importance for the development of all children of a continuous and loving relationship with a parent, nor the additional damage that can be done to an already damaged child by depriving him of a continuing stable relationship with people who love him and whom he can love. All training of child care workers, social workers, health visitors and other field and residential workers is based on these principles which were first set out in the Curtis Report and have recently been endorsed once again in the Court Report.

. . . The fact that a child is mentally handicapped or severely disturbed in no way reduces his basic needs as a child or justifies a quality of care which is in the slightest degree inferior to that which we now consider as a right for non-handicapped children. Indeed, we would argue for a policy of positive discrimination in favour of a group of children who not only have rights as children but special needs and rights as the result of their handicaps. These call for a warm and loving environment which also meets their special developmental needs. These conditions are rarely found in mental handicap hospital.' (64)

The Jay Committee, as we have seen, took the logic of this approach a stage further, by outlining a model of care which saw no place for hospitals at all in the residential scheme of things. So thirty years after the Children Act was passed, the deprivation of one group of children in public care in England was being acknowledged. Just what conditions for them – and other groups of children living away from their family homes – had been like over those thirty years is examined in the next chapter.

Notes

1 Spence, J. C., 'The Care of Children in Hospital', *British Medical Journal*, January 1947, pp. 125–30.

2 *ibid.*

3 Circulars HMC(49)95, HMC(53)17, HMC(56)6, Ministry of Health.

4 *The Welfare of Children in Hospital: Report of the Committee* (Platt Report), Ministry of Health Central Health Services Council, HMSO, 1959, paras 75–80.

5 Circulars HM(61)83, HM(66)18, Ministry of Health.

6 Circular HM(71)50, DHSS and Welsh Office.

7 *Fit for the Future. Report of the Committee on Child Health Services* (Court Report), Cmnd. 6684, HMSO, 1976 para. 4.39.

8 Platt Report, paras 29–32.

9 Circulars HM(67)50, HM(69)4, HM(77)30, Ministry of Health/DHSS, HMSO.

10 Platt Report, HMSO. paras 10 and 15.

11 *ibid.*, paras 35, 100–1, 105.

12 Court Report, para. 4137.

13 *The Health of the School Child: Report of the Chief Medical Officer of the Ministry of Education for the years 1946 and 1947*, HMSO, 1949, pp. 125–8.

14 *ibid.; Education in 1955*, Cmnd. 9785, HMSO, 1956, p. 90.

15 *Report of a survey of long-stay hospital accommodation for children, April 1970*, DHSS, 1970.

16 Platt Report, paras 137–141.

17 Court Report, para. 4.36.

18 *ibid.*, para. 12.42.

19 Platt Report, paras 116–7.

20 Court Report, paras 14.92–4.

21 Circular 5/52, Ministry of Health.

22 *Report of the Royal Commission on the Law Relating to Mental Illness and Mental Deficiency, 1954–7*, Cmnd. 169, HMSO, 1967; *Minutes of Evidence, 14th Day*, p. 152.

23 *Report of the Ministry of Health 1955. Part II. On the State of the Public Health, being the Annual Report of the Chief Medical Officer*, Cmnd. 16, HMSO, 1956, p. 206

24 *Report of the Ministry of Health for the year ended 31st December 1956. Part II. On the State of the Public Health, being the Annual Report of the Chief Medical Officer for the year 1956*, Cmnd. 325, HMSO, 1957, p. 118.

25 *Report of the Ministry of Health for 1957. Part II. On the State of the Public Health, being the Annual Report of the Chief Medical Officer*, Cmnd. 559, HMSO, 1958, p. 221.

26 *Cmnd. 169, Minutes of Evidence, 17th Day*, p. 610.

27 *ibid., 10th Day*, oral questions 2051/2.

28 Circular 26/53, Ministry of Health, HMSO.

29 *Cmnd. 169, Minutes of Evidence, 17th Day*, p. 610.

30 *ibid., 16th Day*, oral question 3059.

31 7 & 8 Eliz. 2 Chapter 72, Part 11, 9(i)2 and Part 11, 10(i)2.

32 *Report of the Ministry of Health, 1960. Part I*, Health and Welfare Services, Cmnd. 1418, HMSO, 1961, para. 14.

33 Circular HM(65)104, DHSS, HMSO.

34 Circular HM(64)4, Ministry of Health.

35 Circular 18/68, Department of Education and Science.

36 *On the State of the Public Health: the Annual Report of the Chief Medical Officer of the DHSS for the year 1969*, HMSO, 1970, pp. 157–161.

37 *Report of the Committee of Enquiry into Allegations of Ill-Treatment of Patients and Other Irregularities at the Ely Hospital, Cardiff*, Cmnd. 3975, HMSO, 1969.

38 *Better Services for the Mentally Handicapped*, DHSS and Welsh Office, Cmnd. 4683, HMSO, 1971, paras 80, 90.40.

39 *ibid.*, paras 158–64.

40 *ibid.*, paras 184–7.

41 *ibid.*, Table 5.

42 *ibid.*, paras 189–92, 241–9.

43 *Hospital Facilities for Children*, annex to Circular HM(71)22, DHSS.

44 Court Report, para. 5.24.

45 *ibid.*, para. 14.76.

46 *ibid.*, para. 14.43, 14.83–6.

47 National Development Group for the Mentally Handicapped, *Mentally Handicapped Children: a Plan for Action*, HMSO, 1977, p. iv, paras 7, 90.

48 Circular HC(78)5, LAC(78)2, DHSS.

49 National Development Group for the Mentally Handicapped, *op. cit.*, paras 8.12.57.

50 Speech to Local Authority Associations Social Services Conference, 25.11.77.

51 *Report of the Committee of Enquiry into Mental Handicap Nursing and Care* (Jay Report), Cmnd. 7468-I. HMSO, 1979, paras 111, 91, 89, 113–23.

52 *ibid.*, paras 144–8.

53 *ibid.*, figure 8, p. 68.

54 *The Function, Scope and Training of Nurses in England and Wales for the Mentally Subnormal*, Royal College of Nursing, 1967, para. 6.

55 *Submission of Views to the Committee of Enquiry into Mental Handicap Nursing and Care*, Campaign for the Mentally Handicapped, *1976*.

56 *Report of the Committee on Nursing*, Cmnd. 5115, HMSO, 1972, paras 563, 284.

57 Court Report, para. 14.87.

58 Jay Report, Chapter 5.

59 Circular HM(72)2, DHSS.

60 *National Health Service, Annual Report of the Hospital Advisory Service to the Secretary of State for Social Services and Secretary of State for Wales for the year 1972*, HMSO, 1973, para. 159.

61 Circular DS 182/73, DHSS.

62. Court Report, para. 14.93.

63 National Development Group for the Mentally Handicapped, *Helping Mentally Handicapped People in Hospital*, DHSS, 1978, para. 3.2.6.

64 *ibid.*, paras 3.2.1, 3.2.3, 3.2.4.

7 Questions of quality

'A good, normal home . . .'

'The organisation is such that the nurses work hurriedly in a chain system, one washing 20 pairs of hands, another combing 20 children's hair and so on ; so it is impossible for a child to have any sustained attention of conversation, let alone affection, from the grown-up.'

'The day begins at 5 a.m. when all the children are awakened by the night nurse. She takes them as a group to the toilet. There all 18 children are sat on chamber pots or toilets in the bathroom. After toileting, they are washed and brought back to the dormitory. Some children go back to sleep, while others lie awake in their beds. At 6 a.m. the night nurse begins to dress the children, working her way round the ward. Because there is little time, and some of the children are slow at dressing, many who could dress themselves are, in fact, dressed by the night nurse.'

The first of these quotations comes from *Whose Children ?*, Lady Allen's pamphlet on the way children in residential homes were looked after at the end of the war ; it describes a residential nursery. The second quotation comes from a study, made some twenty years later, of patterns of care for children in mental handicap institutions. (1) For some children at least it was as if the report of the Curtis Committee and the reforms which stemmed from it had never happened at all.

That is not to say that the Curtis ideal has been reached for the majority of children living away from their own homes ; the pattern of care which has developed since 1948 has not been short of critics. By the end of the 1960s, for instance, an influential group of child care workers was questioning the emphasis on fostering as the best solution for children in care. It deplored the way in which residential homes were seen as 'dumping grounds', as well as the reliance on small group homes which 'aped' family life, while the potential of small grouping within larger establishments was almost ignored. (2) By this time, too, the high rate of breakdown of foster homes was causing alarm. The National Bureau for Co-operation in Child Care concluded its review of the research into fostering like this : 'A very good foster home may offer the affection and security of a real family, but the number of placement breakdowns suggest that at the least several thousands of children each year do not find this ideal substitute family.' (3)

A companion volume on residential child care offered little comfort. 'The picture is not an encouraging one for those who would want the child entrusted to public care to have as nearly as possible the same opportunities as the average child will have in his own family', it concluded. Nearly ten years later, an updated review of the research was quoting this glum conclusion and repeating its predecessor's plea for more research into how best to check the bad effects of residential life on the development and adjustment of children. We still did not know much about what was being done to find alternative homes for children in long-term care, nor about the still crucial problems of finding staff for residential homes. (4)

The people most affected by their elders' uncertainties, the children in care themselves, have recently added their own voice to make clear that neither fostering nor the variety of residential homes now available work for all of them all of the time. (5)

Sometimes, too, handicapped children living away from home can get a better deal than their non-handicapped peers. One study of how children in different institutions spent their weekends found a thoroughly cheerful picture in special residential schools for children with physical handicaps, with plenty of activity and opportunity to participate in the domestic life of the school. (6) By sad contrast, a study of children and young people in children's homes, published three years later in 1974, found very limited weekend activities. Children often said they were bored and spent much of their time watching television or listening to pop music ; there was little evidence of creative activities and few children invited friends in, although many belonged to youth organisations or had the opportunity to go to dances or discos. (7)

So life for children in local authority care has been less fulfilling than child care experts – and often children and young people themselves – would wish, and life for some handicapped children in special establishments has been good. But overall, there can be no doubt at all that many handicapped children in residential care have remained deprived to a degree that the experts in the care of non-handicapped children have in general preferred not to think about.

The rest of this section looks in more detail at the four components the Curtis Committee felt were essential if a substitute home was to 'give the child what he gets from a good, normal home'. Most of the comparisons are between life in children's homes and that in hospitals and there is a reason for this which is in itself revealing : very little work indeed seems to have been done on the way children live in special residential schools.

Affection and personal interest

This was the Curtis Committee's first condition for the substitute home it wanted to see : 'affection and personal interest ; understanding of his defects ; care for his future ; respect for his personality and regard for his self-esteem'. If these qualities are the essential ones, they are also perhaps in some ways the hardest of all to guage. More passes in a glance between a carer and a child or a touch of the hand than ever researchers record in their assessments. But where these qualities are missing, it shows.

Maureen Oswin, in her devastating 1978 study of over 200 severely multiply-handicapped children in 'special care' wards of mental handicap hospitals, found that on average these children received some *five minutes* mothering in ten hours. Children could spend entire days waiting for the next piece of hospital routine to happen to them. In an article based on this study, she had this to say : 'I once saw a six year old handicapped child sitting at a bare table in the ward, weeping silently, and then swirling her fingers around in the tears that fell on the bare table. To see a child sitting alone and playing with her own tears is to be convinced about the reality of maternal deprivation in long-stay hospitals.' (8)

This study showed a real failure to appreciate the children's needs and, indeed, who they were. Children who were learning to play together in a rudimentary way could be arbitrarily separated.

'Many children were frequently anchored all day in wheelchairs, bean-bags or small armchairs, and so had no opportunities for social interaction. The staff did not always seem aware that the ward environment might cause isolation : they did not try to encourage social interaction by different methods of grouping the children, and they did not organise any group-play or have any policy of encouraging the children to interact with each other. It was noticeable that the staff were rarely involved in any social interaction that did take place between the children.' (9)

Although some nurses were clearly devoted to the children, staff attitudes to them could be very negative. 'There's nothing more we can do for them except keep them clean, warm and fed', said one.

'The quality of the children's lives was affected to a great degree with nurses' low expectations : not expecting the children to play, they did not give them the opportunity to do so ; not expecting them to learn to speak, they often failed to speak to them ; not expecting them to learn to feed themselves, they often did not try to teach them to do so.' (10)

When these nurses were asked what their aims were for the children, some replied 'to make them fit well into the adult wards when they grow up, without being a nuisance'. As Maureen Oswin points out, this reflected not only the nurses' limited expectations, but the lack of time they had for children who were a 'nuisance' as well. The most immediate and common expectations of these children were that they should keep fairly still in their wheelchairs, keep fairly quiet, eat quickly and not spit out their food, not smell too badly and sleep well at night. (11)

Given these attitudes, it is perhaps not surprising that in several of the wards 'toys consisted only of a few naked, limbless dolls, torn comics, pieces of broken plastic toys, plastic hammers, toy shopping baskets and "Maxi-bricks" '. In others, the provision could be lavish. In one hospital, for instance, £200 had recently been spent on toys for a new playroom. 'But these toys were kept in an inner cupboard in the new playroom, and the room itself was being used merely as an extension of the rather bare playroom. The more mobile children would roam about it during the evenings, sometimes pushing empty wheelchairs up and down.' (12)

71

The Development Team for the Mentally Handicapped, set up in 1975 as the 'action arm' of the National Development Group to visit and advise hospitals, confirmed this picture three years later from its own visits up and down the country.

'We have encountered a variety of views on the provision of play and leisure equipment and, on occasions, a lack of understanding or appreciation of their value in development, where they are still considered of secondary importance to medical and nursing needs. We still encounter the view that "toys will only be broken" which, although true of all children, is used here as a reason for not providing them. In many hospitals, toys, stimulating mobiles and pictures are available, but often they are locked away in cupboards out of reach of the children for most of the day or so placed that the children cannot see them.' (13)

Children could be placed in front of a television, irrespective of what was being shown, sometimes simply staring at a test card. (14)

The contrasts with children's homes are stark, as King, Raynes and Tizard found in the early 1960s in a comparative study of two large local authority children's homes, a paediatric hospital with a number of wards on which children had been living for a long time, and a mental handicap hospital. In both the hospitals, they found a social distance between staff and children : 'child management tended to be rigid and inflexible in routine, children were regimented in groups and made to queue and wait around without anything to do for lengthy periods and in general had few personal possessions or opportunities for self-expression or initiative'. Children's homes were very different. In these, 'child management' was on the whole oriented to the children and not to the demands of the institution ; the children were free to participate or not in various activities ; they could show initiative, have possessions and be alone if they wanted to be ; social distance between staff and children was lessened through their sharing of living space. (15)

Just what differences 'institution-oriented' and 'child-oriented' patterns of care could mean to children was clearly illustrated in this study. The differences began at the very start of the day. Children in the mental handicap hospital had to be up, potted and ready for the day before the day-staff came on duty – which could mean a start to getting up as early as 4 or 5 a.m. Children in the paediatric hospital got up at about 6 a.m. In only one ward of the mental handicap hospital were children allowed in the day-room before the day-staff came on ; in others, they just sat about in or on their beds, unless a nurse took the initiative to provide some toys or books. Children in the local authority homes, by contrast, got up between 6.45 and 7.30 a.m. according to when they had set off for school, and came down to breakfast as soon as they were ready ; the housemother or assistant helped children who needed assistance with dressing. Both staff and children would have a lie-in at weekends.

The shape of mealtimes – that cement of any community – differed too. In the hospitals, meals arrived ready-prepared from central kitchens. Children rarely saw any food being prepared ; even when snacks and drinks were prepared on the ward, few were allowed to watch this. Children could be sat at table for twenty minutes waiting for the meals to arrive. The staff were only allowed to share a meal with the children on Christmas Day. In the children's homes, the housemothers and assistants prepared all the meals and the children were expected to help ; at least one member of staff shared each meal with them.

After each meal, the children in the mental handicap hospital were taken to the lavatory en bloc. There was often a conveyor-belt system : one nurse would toilet children while another washed and dried them. In about half the wards, too, all the children were kept in the bathroom until the routine was complete for the whole group. The conveyor-belt system was used here too. In the children's homes, for a start, there were lavatories which offered a normal degree of privacy – which were never found in the hospitals. Although a third of the children in the homes needed help with washing or bathing, this was always offered individually.

The day ended as differently as it had begun. In the hospitals, some children started going to bed at 4 p.m. In the children's homes, bed time varied with the children's ages and was between 6.30 and 10 p.m. Staff in these homes would read to the younger children in bed. This never happened in the hospitals.

The contrasts can be multiplied. Children in the local authority homes had their own clothes ; none of the children in the mental handicap hospital had all their own, most being provided from a central store 'according to approximate size'. Children in the homes could use their house and gardens more or less as they wished ; children in the hospitals were faced with many 'out of bounds' areas and had little scope to explore without escort. Children in the homes had a special fuss made of them on their birthdays, with a tea-party and cards and a present. Children in the mental handicap hospital got a special tea 'if they were thought to benefit' – but no present.

None of these contrasts had anything to do with the fact that some of the children were handicapped and some were not. King, Raynes and Tizard also compared local authority homes for severely mentally handicapped children to mental handicap hospital wards. They found that all the local homes had 'child-oriented' patterns of care and all the hospital units had patterns which were 'institution-oriented'. (16)

The differences between the lives of children in homes and those in hospitals were stark then. They remain so. At the beginning of the 1970s, Maureen Oswin charted what life was like at weekends for children in different institutions. Those in mental handicap hospitals and wards for the physically handicapped shared a routine of sad dreariness – a deprivation made the more striking by its contrast with the cheerful activities of children with *equally severe* physical handicap in special residential schools. (17) In 1976, the Health (formerly the Hospital) Advisory Service confirmed the picture. While it found well-organised play in some of the long-stay wards for children with physical disabilities and phychiatric problems that it visited, in others it found cupboards full of unused toys and unused beds where playspace could have been. 'It is of considerable concern', it said, 'that when no school or occupation was available, for example in the evenings or at weekends, children were sometimes dressed and lying on their beds doing nothing – because, as one said, "I have been reading for the last three hours".' There was too little creative activity available for some of the older children, particularly in the evenings and at weekends'. (18)

Far too little seems to have changed since King, Raynes and Tizard did their work. In 1978, Maureen Oswin still found that the needs of the institution could be taking precedence over those of the children. 'Lacking guidelines on how to care for multiply-handicapped children, and lacking specialist support, the special-care ward nurses appear to be merely ticking over in an endlessly repetitive performance of routine domestic tasks', she reported. 'Getting ahead of routines' was one of their characteristics :

'The almost ceremonial manner in which the staff of some wards made these early preparations for bed-times, bath-times, and meal-times gave a structure to the work but hardly enhanced the standards of child care. Indeed, it appeared that the children had become mere appendages to a policy of saving time. A poignant example of this urge to get ahead of routines was seen in one hospital on Christmas Eve ; after the children had been put to bed, some of their Christmas presents were opened by the staff and put away in order to save time on Christmas Day.' (19)

When she made her study, she found some children still sat ready for their meals up to forty minutes before these arrived. Staff were still discouraged from sharing a mealtime with the children by having to pay for it ; the National Development Group (NDG) recorded its surprise that in 1978 the DHSS still did not recognise that sharing meals was an integral part of the staff's work. (20) In that year, the NDG was still having to recommend that each child in a mental handicap hospital had his or her own clothes and toys and was enabled to share ordinary activities of childhood as far as possible. It was still noting that there were not enough staff to tell children a goodnight story, to sing to them or play individually with them. It was still noting that some children had their last meal of the day between 3.30 and 4 p.m. 'for the convenience of the system', (21) and the Development Team was still noting that some children were being got up in the morning at 6 a.m. or even earlier. (22) The NDG was still having to emphasise that each child's self-esteem should be encouraged by birthday celebrations. 'Many hospitals recognised this, but in some cases birthday cards, presents, etc, are sometimes consigned to the staffroom or somewhere other than the child's immediate surroundings because of the risk of "interference from other children." ' (23)

Many of these failures in child care could be put down to the deadening effect of gross staff shortages. Maureen Oswin, for instance, found sixteen multiply-handicapped children being cared for by one fifteen-year-old volunteer. It was, in 1978, quite common for groups of up to thirty severely handicapped children to be cared for by two or three members of staff. The National Development Group was categoric :

'Even with the best will in the world and the most enlightened leadership, staff in these conditions will end each day in a state of near exhaustion as a result of the sheer physical tasks involved in feeding, cleaning and toileting the children in their care. Very little else is possible with staff that are grossly overworked and unsupported, or staff who are physically and emotionally exhausted.'

It recommended that no less than one member of staff should be available to two profoundly or severely handicapped children during the day. (24) The Jay Committee agreed with this, adding that there should be one member of staff on duty for every three less handicapped children. (25)

But it is not just a question of more staff. We have seen how those there are either trained in nursing or relate to that approach to care. King, Raynes and Tizard warned that 'even well-staffed units can be run in an institutionally-orientated manner if the staff are not properly organised and if they do not receive the right kind of training'. They found that it was where the head of the unit was trained in child care rather than in nursing that children were on the receiving end of a 'child-oriented' rather than an 'institution-oriented' regime. (26) By 1978, the National Development Group was recommending that the head of each unit for mentally handicapped children in hospital should be someone with specific training in child care. (27) The Jay Committee, as we have seen, wanted training in child care for caring staff as well. (28)

Just what differences patterns of care could make to the development of children had been dramatically demonstrated by Jack Tizard himself as early as the end of the 1950s. His 'Brooklands' experiment took sixteen severely mentally handicapped children from a ward at Fountain Hospital to an ordinary house. There they were offered, instead of the 'unending formal lessons in sense-training, toilet-training, social training, speech training and the like', an educational and care regime based on the Home Office's 1955 guidance for residential nurseries. Although it took the whole of the experiment's first year to find stable enough staffing to set up nursery groups for the children, by the end of that year they had changed dramatically. When they arrived, they were mostly mute, unable to play with others, to bear frustrations or show any preference between adults ; they were liable to hit, sometimes to bite, subject to violent rages. At the end of the year, they were a group who enjoyed playing, talked a fair amount between themselves, were affectionate, happy, interested in what they were doing, for the most part docile and easy to manage, fond of the staff as the staff were of them. 'If the contrast sounds too good to be true', said Tizard, 'it is because the child itself has exceeded our expectations.' (29) And the improvement was maintained.

The Brooklands experiment became famous. Yet in 1978, Maureen Oswin was still showing the effects of institutional life on severely handicapped children. The ones she studied had many bizarre habits – like sucking their hands, or clothes, making monotonous singing noises, banging doors, spinning the wheels of over-turned wheelchairs, tearing up paper, hitting or poking at their own ears, eyes, nose, mouth or head. All these habits, as she says, might be described as the typical behaviour of severely mentally handicapped children. Yet these children were also severely deprived of mothering and play ; their behaviours could be aggravated by this, the only way they had of filling the time. And these activities could work against them. 'As ward staff rarely have opportunities to observe the children away from the ward, many of them come to believe that peculiar behaviour patterns are entirely due to mental handicap.' (30)

Given the affection and personal interest, understanding and respect that the Curtis Committee saw as essential to a good substitute home, severely mentally handicapped children can develop far more than even those who care for them often believe. But in 1978, over 4000 of these children and some 1500 others with severe physical handicaps were deprived of their right to that good substitute home in the bleak surroundings of long-stay hospitals.

Stability

This was the second of the Curtis Committee's conditions for a good substitute home : 'stability ; the feeling that [the child] can expect to remain with those who will continue to care for him till he goes out into the world on his own feet'.

And this is a condition which has rarely been met. By the end of the 1960s, nearly 40% of children's homes had had at least two heads in the past five years and a third of all staff left each year – more than in any other category of residential home. At that time, it was in fact special boarding schools, including approved schools and remand homes, which had the best track record in hiring trained staff and keeping them. Overall, some 38% of 'care staff' had some formal qualification and the turnover of staff in general was a quarter in each year ; only 27% of these schools had had more than one head in the past five years. (31) By 1975, it seemed that rather less than a third of all full-time staff in children's homes left each year. (32) Barbara Tizard has pointed out what this can mean to the individual child in care : on average, twenty-four members of staff had looked after the children in one group of residential nurseries for at least a week since the children had been there. (33)

But if turnover of staff has been a constant problem in children's homes, it has been an even worse one in mental handicap hospitals. King, Raynes and Tizard estimated that in some of these hospitals, immature and handicapped children might have to adjust to as many as one hundred different adults or more in the course of a single year. (34) The problem in these hospitals has been the practice of rotating staff through the wards as needed rather than attaching them to a specific ward and group of children. Maureen Oswin found in her 1978 study that although senior staff were permanently attached to the wards, with a small nucleus of other permanent staff, the majority were 'floaters' – students, pupils or cadets on short-term placements. In some hospitals, only a quarter of the staff were permanently attached to the wards, and most of them were part-time. (35)

As we have seen, the DHSS has recommended 'patient assignment' in the care of all children living for long periods in hospital – which means that a group of staff is permanently assigned to look after a given group of children. Where this system had been adopted, the Development Team reported in 1978, staff found that they could offer better care to the children and that the system was not as hard to work as they had imagined. (36) But this way of caring was by no means general by then. In the same year, the National Development Group was still reiterating the principle that no member of staff should be taken from a children's ward to help out in other parts of the hospital. (37)

Making the best of abilities

This was the third of the Curtis Committee's conditions for a good substitute home : 'opportunity for making the best of [the child's] abilities and aptitudes, whatever they may be, as such opportunity is made available to the child in the normal home'.

As we have seen earlier in this section, children living in hospital have often completely lacked this essential opportunity.They have been left bored and listless; they have not been taught to play, to eat unaided, to dress themselves. They have even lacked the mothering which is so vital to any child's development. If they are severely mentally handicapped, they have often lived with staff who themselves sadly lack guidance and encouragement in how to help them develop, who are exhausted by the sheer physical effort of caring for them.

The lack of opportunity can be even more basic than that. In 1971, the Hospital Advisory Service had noted its concern about the lack of physiotherapy for multiply-handicapped children, which could lead to serious and grotesque deformities which were irremediable by adolescence. Maureen Oswin, in her 1978 study, found that only seventy-five of the children were getting physiotherapy. 'Some of the cerebrally palsied children were pitifully deformed ; their bodies were so screwed up that it was difficult to see where their ribs began and their hips ended ; some of these children could never sit up, they could only lie in twisted positions on their sides and their only view of the world was from one eye. It is possible that their deformities had worsened through lack of early physiotherapy help'. (38) In some cases, corrective surgery had not been done because orthopaedic surgeons had been reluctant and mental handicap consultants had not pressed for the child's rights.

None of the children were getting speech therapy, although this could have helped many to learn to overcome their eating difficulties. Psychologists were involved with them in only one of the eight hospitals – and there were not enough staff for their programmes to be taken up on the wards. Children were often using inappropriate wheelchairs ; other aids were in short supply. The majority had not had their sensory handicaps fully assessed, although it was thought that about half of them, for instance, might have a hearing loss. Even elementary health care could be lacking. In five of the eight hospitals, the children suffered from 'the poverty conditions of the nineteenth century' – chronic catarrh, runny noses, sore eyes, skin diseases, chronic recurring stomach upsets, bad teeth and worms. (39)

The designation of the places in which these children lived as 'special care wards' had a horrible irony, for special care is exactly what they were deprived of. For very many, the opportunity of making the most of their abilities simply did not exist.

A small group and homely environment

This was the fourth of the Curtis Committee's conditions for a good substitute home : 'a share in the common life of a small group of people in a homely environment'.

We have seen the huge impetus for replacing large institutions for children in care with small homes, for those who were not fostered, in the early years of the new children's service. We have seen how guidance on special boarding schools picked up on many of the elements of small group living and domestic environment that the Home Office was urging. We have seen too the completely different approach of the health service to providing places for children to live in ; its comparatively few suggestions for reform have most often been made in the context of a prevailing service which catered for children and adults alike. These different approaches have made for very different environments for children.

Here is a description of Fountain Hospital, the largest in the country to cater specifically for mentally handicapped children, almost a decade after the Curtis Committee made its report. There were up to sixty beds in a ward, which meant severe overcrowding and a lack of personal attention ; harassed nurses were constantly coping with emergencies.

'The lack of facilities made work very difficult. The sanitary arrangements for so many incontinent children were primitive. The wooden floorboards were uneven and inclined to splinter and in some wards it was impossible to get rid of the smell of urine and faeces. Cupboard space was inadequate and there was nowhere for patients' possessions. It was difficult to keep toys on the ward. The playgrounds were of asphalt ; the school rooms were very small and overcrowded and lacking in equipment. The staff quarters were close to the wards and very noisy. In these and many other ways, the physical environment of an old, former fever hospital which had been adapted for a purpose for which it was not suited, made the care of physically and mentally handicapped children a very great burden.' (40)

It was not for another decade, as we have seen, that the Ministry of Health recommended improvements in such hospitals, among which was the suggestion that no ward for children should have more than twenty places. Yet a major survey of mental handicap hospitals at the end of the 1960s found one children's ward of eighty children, with only one day/dining-room. 'Staff had to choose between returning children to their dormitories after meals or clearing away, stacking the furniture and wiping the floor while other staff "potted" and cleaned up the children and attempted to keep them away from the debris of the meal.' In another children's ward, in the middle of the afternoon, 'fifty older children [were] wandering around aimlessly or sitting making noises, despite the fact that there were six staff actually on duty in the ward. There were no toys, books, games, pictures, or ornaments in evidence and the staff stood around talking to each other.' (41)

At this time two-thirds of the adults and children in mental handicap hospitals were living in wards of over forty beds ; in only a third of them did inhabitants have some personal clothing. (42) Official persuasion to bring down the size of children's wards to twenty places has had its effect, yet by 1975, 7% of children in mental handicap hospitals were still living in larger wards than this. (43) There have been efforts to create small living groups within these wards, although it is not possible to say how widespread this practice is. In 1978, the National Development Group was recommending that there should be no more than six children in a group on a hospital ward. (44) The following year, as we have seen, the Jay Committee found this the maximum number for its local homes. (45)

Even where new buildings have been provided, the small groups and homely environment which have been an essential component of child care since 1948 may be completely lacking in hospital. The report on Normansfield Hospital in 1978, for instance, showed that there the chidren's ward houses thirty boys and girls. 'All the basic facilities are here, but the place was of stark clinical appearance which deprived the patients of any individuality. No separate playrooms were available and there was a pen in one corner in which a few youngsters were incarcerated.' This report underlined the deadening interaction of a bad environment and poor care. 'The nursing staff appeared to place an unnecessary emphasis on total observation and were not involving themselves in patients' activities.' Visitors to this ward in 1975 found appalling standards of hygiene, including filthy lavatories, dust and dirt. (46) In 1978, too, the Development Team was reporting 'the most appalling buildings and cramped conditions without even adequate facilities for washing, bathing or storage of clothing' in other children's wards. (47)

So mentally handicapped children living in hospital have been offered few chances of the small group living and homely environment that Curtis wanted to see. There have been further contrasts between different groups of children living away from their own homes. A 'homely environment' has to do with furnishing and organisation within the living unit. But it also has to do with what you see when you look out of the window and how near you are to familiar places. This in turn has to do with the *overall* size of the unit in which you live, for the larger it is the more likely you are to get your social life within it and the less likely you are to live near places you know. Here again there have been sharp contrasts between what has been offered to children in children's homes and to those in other residential places.

A census of all residential provision for children in 1971 found that the average size of a children's home was 15 places. At the same time, however, the average size of a special boarding school was 61 places, of an independent school for handicapped children, 49, of a local authority home for mentally handicapped children, 18, and of voluntary and private provision for these children, 27. Hospital units for mentally handicapped children, however, had an average of 113 places – and that usually in the context of a far larger institution catering for adults as well. (48) So while children in the care of local authorities have at least a chance of being near familiar places, those in residential schools have much less chance – particularly as these often cater for a very specific disability – and those in mental handicap hospitals have very little chance at all.

Site has as important a bearing on the quality of life for children in a residential establishment as does overall size, and here again different groups of children have been offered different places to live. We have seen how at the end of the war, the Ministry of Education was pressing the advantages of large country mansions on authorities looking for new special boarding schools. So, by the end of the 1960s, when 90% of children's homes were within twenty minutes' walk of shops and other community facilities, this was true of only two-thirds of boarding special schools. (49) The advantages of country air can wear thin for an urban child and problems of contact with the local community and of staffing are likely to increase if an establishment is not easily accessible to its local community.

The deliberate policy of siting colonies for the mentally handicapped away from centres of population has been increasingly foiled in recent years as urban overspill housing has crept out to meet them, and their isolation is often now that of the inward-looking artificial community rather than of geography ; nevertheless, many are still extraordinarily difficult to reach without a car.

Children who are in hospital because of long-term physical handicaps also suffer from isolation. 'The concept of "convalescent type" small hospitals situated in beautiful countryside, miles away from anywhere, seems outmoded', the Health Advisory Service has commented. 'The staffing of such small outlying units is usually hazardous, not only in maintaining numbers but also quality of staff.' (50) Recent suggestions that mentally handicapped children should live on the sites of general hospitals have added a new hazard to their lives. There is nothing like a hospital for persuading outsiders that the inhabitants are 'sick' – why else, after all, would they be there ? – and so out of the normal social running.

We have seen that the early principles of homes for children have been modified in recent years ; the 1971 guidance suggests a unit of up to to 50 places, if there is education on site, in living groups of 8 to 12. (51) Guidance on a hospital unit for mentally handicapped children, issued in the same year, shows that in some ways the two services have at last come closer together. This envisages a 'home' for 24 mentally handicapped children, living in three groups of 8. But while the design guide for the community home emphasises the importance of siting this in an urban area with good public transport, the one for the hospital unit chooses a site on the grounds of a district general hospital, linked to an adult mental handicap unit with 96 places. This site is real enough ; it is in Sheffield, part of the DHSS's only excursion into the joint planning of an area service for mentally handicapped people. (52) The siting of the home could hardly be more abnormal. Not only is it part of a hospital complex, but it is administratively linked with a residential service for mentally handicapped adults – which the children can conveniently join, presumably, as they grow up. It was left to the National Development Group to urge, in 1978, that whenever possible hospitals should provide their residential accommodation for children right outside the hospital site, (53) and to the Jay Committee, the following year, to emphasise that all residential accommodation should be local to the child's family home. (54)

Different residential settings for different groups of children have, then, varied enormously in the extent to which they met the Curtis Committee's recommendations for achieving a good substitute home. The ways in which these settings have been monitored have been very different too : the rest of this chapter looks at the different methods of quality control.

Quality control

Different settings for children living away from their own homes have, since the war, been differently supervised and monitored. Until 1971, the Home Office backed its memoranda and guidance with the visits of its inspectorate to both local authority and voluntary homes. Under the Children and Young Persons Act 1969, all homes which come under regional planning committees are governed by the Community Homes Regulations (SI 1972 No. 319) which replaced earlier regulations tailored to each set of homes. Overall responsibility for these homes and for voluntary ones which remain outside the regional planning system lies with the DHSS. Its regional social work service has taken over the functions of the Home Office inspectorate ; there is no ruling about the frequency of visits.

Boarding schools for handicapped children, like other schools, have to be registered under the 1944 Education Act. To achieve registration, they have to meet minimum requirements for premises and staff. All LEA schools and special voluntary schools are also recognised as efficient by definition ; most independent schools are also recognised, after a decision by the Secretary of State, following a report from one of its inspectors (HMIs). These inspectors have the right of entry to all schools and are responsible for both educational and boarding facilities. If a school does not take notice of an HMI recommendation for improvements, the Secretary of State can serve a 'notice of complaint' requiring it to do certain things within a certain period of time. Recognition may also be withdrawn from an independent school. After the 1970 Education Act came into force, bringing severely mentally handicapped children for the first time within the scope of the educational system, a few establishments which had been homes for severely mentally handicapped children became schools. They did not lose their status of 'homes', however, but have taken dual registration. By 1978, the system of recognition was under review.

While both homes for children in care and special boarding schools are safeguarded by inspectorates which can work to national standards of what is acceptable care, children in establishments for the mentally handicapped have no such protection. Local authority homes for mentally handicapped children, even though they are run by the same departments as community homes, are not subject to the Community Homes Regulations. In fact, they are subject to no regulations at all and the question of their inspection is not covered in any legislation.

Private and voluntary homes for mentally handicapped children come under different arrangements again. Unlike other voluntary children's homes, which are registered under the 1948 Children Act if they are not part of the community homes system, these are registered either under the 1948 National Assistance Act and 1959 Mental Health Act, and governed by one set of regulations (SI 2000) ; or under the 1959 Mental Health Act as mental nursing homes and governed by another set of regulations (SI 1999). These regulations are concerned mainly with material standards, although they also cover staffing and medical and dental services. What they do not do is to impose any requirement on the authority registering the home to make any assessment of standards of care. In this they are less effective than the regulations covering community homes for children in care, which oblige the responsible body to 'make proper provision for the care, treatment and control of the children accommodated'.

The serious inadequacies of the system of registering private and voluntary homes for mentally handicapped children, and in the supervision of children in them, were pinpointed by the Harvie study group in 1974. This had been set up by the DHSS after the death of a child in a private home and revealed some very disquieting facts about this whole area of care. Children could be sent to these homes and then virtually abandoned by all authorities ; the study group found one child who had not been visited at all for four years. No specific responsibility for visiting and supervising is placed on either the social services department which places the child or the one that registers the home it is in ; the study group found it essential that they sorted out this responsibility between them. (55)

Many of the problems surrounding these private and voluntary homes, the study group found, had to do with the inadequacy of the regulations that govern them. It came across instances of authorities which were gravely concerned with the standards in homes and yet felt the regulations would not allow them to intervene. The study group wanted to see new regulations to govern these homes, which brought them into line with those covering community homes for children in care. (56)

Other problems arose from the fact that many handicapped children in residential care away from their own home areas are not legally 'in care' at all. So they are deprived of the protection of legislation governing children in care – including a six-monthly review on their progress. The study group wanted this sort of protection extended to mentally handicapped children in private and voluntary residential homes. This report was commended to local authorities by the DHSS when it first came out. There has been no official word on its recommendations since.

The standards of care of children in hospital were from the start of the NHS the responsibility of hospital management committees (HMCs), through them the regional hospital boards and through them the Minister of Health himself. The official inquiries into conditions in mental handicap hospitals, starting with that into Ely Hospital, published in 1969, showed clearly enough that their HMCs had failed most miserably in their duties.

The Committee of Enquiry into Ely Hospital pointed out that almost everything it criticised in the running of the hospital – standards of nursing care and discipline, staff training and establishments, investigation of complaints, overcrowding and standards of amenity on the wards, lack of activity for the residents – fell more or less within the responsibility of the HMC, half of whose members were over sixty years old and a quarter over seventy. 'One of the most disquieting features of this scene at Ely', said the report, 'is summarised in the following answers given by a senior member of the HMC at an early stage of our proceedings :

Q : Have you always been perfectly happy about what you have seen here ?
A : Perfectly.
Q : In fact, you did a long inspection of the hospital yesterday ?
A : Yes.'

The HMC and its officers and advisors, the Committee concluded, must accept 'the principal responsibility for the shortcomings identified ; an ineffective system of administration ; the effective isolation of Ely from the mainstream of progress and the absence of any well-informed stimulation towards an improvement of standards'. (58)

The Farleigh Hospital Committee of Enquiry found much the same thing. 'The reports of the HMC on its visits were surprisingly uncritical of conditions at the hospital and without mention of the real difficulties faced by staff. They seemed to us to show that members were unaware of new developments which were taking place in the care of the mentally handicapped both at home and abroad. They spoke almost uniformly of the high standard of hygiene and physical care at Farleigh. We conclude that the standards by which the hospital was judged were its own internal standards.' (59) The Committee of Enquiry into South Ockenden Hospital completes the dreary litany.The regional hospital board, the Committee found, had made little effort to discover how patients were cared for or to eliminate any defects ; the HMC 'took a restricted view of its duty.' (60)

In 1974, with the reorganisation of the National Health Service, HMCs were abolished and responsibility for running hospitals passed to area health authorities. Community health councils were set up to keep a watching brief on the development of health services and represent the consumer interest in a service now dominated by professional management.

Professional management, it transpired, could be as inadequate as that by ordinary citizens. The Committee of Enquiry into Normansfield Hospital, set up in the aftermath of an unprecedented strike of nurses which endangered the health and welfare of residents, found an almost total collapse of morale among staff at the hospital. Its 1978 report found that

'the main cause for the shortfall in patient care and development was not lack of finance but a failure of duty by the Area Health Authority (and in particular by the Area Management Team). The Regional Health Authority failed adequately to monitor the work of the Area Health Authority and did not ensure that its policy in relation to the delivery of care to the mentally handicapped was carried out. There was a significant failure in general to implement the policy laid down in the Government White Paper *Better Services for the Mentally Handicapped.'* (61)

The report on Ely Hospital, as we have seen, triggered a new kind of monitoring of the performance of mental handicap hospitals – the Hospital (later the Health) Advisory Service. The first draft of the scheme for the National Health Service had in fact envisaged a 'hospital inspectorate', but this idea was dropped. (62) Over the years, it was resurrected from time to time – notably when *Sans Everything* revealed the extent of deprivation of old people living in hospital. (63) And it was resurrected again, this time by the then Secretary of State for Health and Social Services, Richard Crossman, when he first read the report on Ely Hospital. He decided that he could only publish it and survive politically if he announced at the same time 'necessary changes in policy, including the adoption by the Ministry and the regional hospital boards of a system of inspectorates, central and regional, such as there are in almost every other Ministry and such as the Health Service has never yet permitted itself'. (64)

It had long been part of prevailing mythology that the medical profession would never accept an inspectorate and Crossman found himself embattled with his senior civil servants over the issue. At times it seemed that the civil servants were themselves determined to scupper the idea ; on one occasion they simply removed from a draft proposal Crossman's central idea of making the new body directly responsible to the Secretary of State, substituting their own of responsibility to the regions. When Crossman met leaders of the medical profession to discuss the proposal, he found that they had been wrongly briefed and had the impression that he wanted an inspectorate of civil servants rather than of professional workers on secondment. In the end, the 'Ministry bigwigs' beat him down and he settled for a professional 'scrutiny or advisory service', but insisted that this should be completely independent of the administration of the Department of Health. (65)

This was introduced as the Hospital Advisory Service, which in its first year did a quick gallop throught the country's mental handicap hospitals, making reports which were not vouchsafed to the public. Its promised follow-up visit was abandoned in favour of the pressing needs of geriatric hospitals, for its brief was to cover all long-stay hospitals. Later, as the Health Advisory Service, its remit was extended to cover the whole range of health and social service provision for all long-stay groups. It never, however, got back to provision for mentally handicapped children or adults at all.

Instead, the Development Team, set up in 1975, became responsible for visiting places where mentally handicapped children and adults lived. Unlike the Hospital Advisory Service, it could only visit by invitation for the first three years of its life. Following the report on Normansfield Hospital in 1978, however, its remit was extended to visits at the direction of the Secretary of State.

None of these efforts to monitor the hospital service for mentally handicapped people has proved always strong enough for the job. The Hospital Advisory Service had in fact visited Normansfield Hospital twice in its early years ; six years after its second visit, conditions were revealed to be deplorable. The Development Team's standards have themselves caused considerable disquiet. In one of its few reports on individual services to be made public, for instance, its comments on the 'quality of life' on a children's ward ran to one short paragraph. It comments on the need for more and constant staff, and then goes on : 'The staff were, however, concerned about the children's well-being. They were friendly and there was some hand to hand contact. They addressed children by their christian names.' (66) Would that have been enough for Curtis ?

Even the Ministry of Health's own efforts to monitor the services for which its Minister was responsible could be remarkably half-hearted. During the battles within the Department of Health on whether or not the report on Ely Hospital should be published in its shocking entirety, it emerged that the Ministry had been sending its own visitors to the hospital for years. Their last report, three or four years before that of the Committee of Enquiry, was, according to Crossman, 'a deplorable report, admitting scandalous conditions, bad nursing' – in fact, the basis of everything that the Committee of Enquiry had confirmed. What had happened to this internal report ? *It had been filed.* (67)

Some Ministry of Health habits die hard. When asked, at the time of Lady Allen's campaign for an enquiry, what reports were made on children in his Ministry's care, the Minister of Health replied : 'Reports are of course made, and are placed in the appropriate file.' (68)

Services to different groups of children living away from their own home, then, have been differently monitored and with differing degrees of efficacy, according to which government department has been responsible for them. While both the Ministry of Education and, until 1971, the Home Office, had strong central inspectorates, the Ministry of Health had no such body and only after the report on Ely Hospital had revealed how bad conditions could be did it make belated efforts to find alternatives. At the same time, the extent to which different groups of children were offered standards of care approaching the Curtis ideal varied enormously. The next chapter examines how this situation has been allowed to continue over thirty years.

Notes

1 King, R., Raynes, N. and Tizard, J., *Patterns of Residential Care*, Routledge and Kegan Paul, 1971, p. 97.

2 Kahan, B. and Banner, G., *The Residential Task in Child Care*, 2nd edn, Residential Care Association, 1972.

3 Dinnage, R. and Kelmer Pringle, M., *Foster Home Care, Facts and Fallacies,* National Bureau for Co-operation in Child Care, 1967, p. 21.

4 Prosser, H., *Perspectives on Residential Child Care*, NFER Publishing Company, 1974, pp. 22–3.

5 *Who Cares ?*, National Children's Bureau, 1977.

6 Oswin, M., *The Empty Hours*, Allen Lane, 1971.

7 Brown, J. and Solomon, D., 'Leisure Time Interests of Children in Residential Homes,' *Residential Social Work*, vol. 14, no. 7, 1974, p. 246.

8 Oswin, M., in *Child : care, health and development*, vol. 3, 1977, pp. 349–335.

9 Oswin, M., *Children Living in Long-stay Hospitals*, Spastics International Medical Publications/Heinemann Medical Books, 1978, pp. 118–124.

10 *ibid.*, p. 90.

11 *ibid.*, p. 91.

12 *ibid.*, p. 125.

13 Development Team for the Mentally Handicapped, *First Report : 1976–1977*, DHSS, HMSO, 1978, para. 48.

14 *Helping Mentally Handicapped People in Hospital : a Report to the Secretary of State for Social Services by the National Development Group for the Mentally Handicapped*, DHSS, 1978, para. 3.2.4.

15 King, R., Raynes, N. and Tizard, J., *supra.*

16 *ibid.*

17 Oswin, M., 1971.

18 National Health Service, *Annual Report of the Health Advisory Service to the Secretary of State for Social Services and Secretary of State for Wales for the year 1975*, HMSO, 1976, para. 44 *e.s.*

19 Oswin, M., 1978, p. 87.

20 National Development Group, *supra*, para. 3,2.26.

21 *ibid.*, paras 3.2.8, 3.2.4.

22 Development Team for the Mentally Handicapped, *supra*, para. 47.

23 National Development Group, *supra*, para. 3.2.30.

24 *ibid.*, para. 3.2.8.

25 *Report of the Committee of Enquiry into Mental Handicap Nursing and Care* (Jay Report), Cmnd. 7468-I, HMSO, 1979, para. 175.

26 King, R., Raynes, N. and Tizard, J., *supra*.

27 National Development Group, *supra*, para. 3.2.17.

28 Jay Report, para. 222.

29 Tizard, J., 'Residential Care of Mentally Handicapped Children,' in *British Medical Journal*, 1960, pp. 1041–6.

30 Oswin, M., 1978, pp. 103–7

31 National Institute for Social Work Training, *Caring for People*, Allen and Unwin, 1967, pp. 74, 94.

32 *Personal Social Services Local Authority Statistics*, s/f 76/5, DHSS, 1976.

33 Tizard, B., 'Varieties of Residential Nursery Experience' in Tizard, J., Sinclair, I. and Clarke, R. (eds), *Varieties of Residential Experience*, Routledge and Kegan Paul, 1975.

34 King, R., Raynes, N. and Tizard, J., *supra*, p. 195.

35 Oswin, M., 1978, p. 77.

36 Development Team for the Mentally Handicapped, *supra*, para. 46.

37 National Development Group for the Mentally Handicapped, *supra*, para. 3.2.25.

38 Oswin, M., 1977.

39 Oswin, M., 1978.

40 Tizard, J., *Community Services for the Mentally Handicapped*, Oxford University Press, 1964, p. 79.

41 Morris, P., *Put Away*, Routledge and Kegan Paul, 1969, pp. 80, 170.

42 *ibid.*

43 *The Facilities and Services of Mental Illness and Mental Handicap Hospitals in England, 1975*, DHSS Statistical and Research-Report Series, no. 19, HMSO, 1977.

44 National Development Group, *supra*, 3.2.24.

45 Jay Report, para. 114.

46 *Report of the Committee of Inquiry into Normansfield Hospital*, DHSS, Cmnd. 7357, HMSO, 1978, Section XIV, para. 25 ; Section VI, para. 7.

47 Development Team for the Mentally Handicapped, *supra*, para. 44.

48 Moss, P., 'Residential Care of Children – a General View', in Tizard, J., Sinclair, I. and Clarke, R., *supra*.

49 National Institute for Social Work Training, *supra*, pp. 74,94.

50 Health Advisory Service, *supra*, para. 45.

51 *Community Homes Design Guide*, DHSS, Advisory Council on Child Care, HMSO, 1971.

52 *A Hospital Unit for Children (Sheffield Type A)*, DHSS, 1973.

53 National Development Group, *supra*, para. 3.2.22.

54 Jay Report, paras. 91, 114, 115.

55 *Mentally Handicapped Children in Residential Care : the Report of a Study Group appointed by the Secretary of State for Social Services*, HMSO, 1974, paras 39, 75.

56 *ibid.*, paras 96, 98.

57 *ibid.*, para. 40.

58 *Report of the Committee of Enquiry into Allegations of Ill-Treatment of Patients and Other Irregularities at the Ely Hospital, Cardiff*, Cmnd. 3875, HMSO, 1969, paras 402, 514.

59 *Report of the Farleigh Hospital Committee of Enquiry*, Cmnd. 4557, HMSO, 1971, para. 42.

60 *Report of the Committee of Inquiry into South Ockenden Hospital*, HMSO, 1974, para. 489.

61 *Report of the Committee of Inquiry into Normansfield Hospital*, DHSS, Cmnd. 7357, 'Principal Conclusions of the Enquiry', para. 2.

62 *A National Health Service*, Ministry of Health and Dept. of Health for Scotland, Cmd. 6502, HMSO, 1944, p. 24.

63 Robb, B. (ed.), *Sans Everything – a Case to Answer*, Nelson, 1967.

64 Crossman, R., *The Diaries of a Cabinet Minister*, vol. 3, Hamish Hamilton and Jonathan Cape, 1977, p. 409.

65 *ibid.*, p. 418.

66 Development Team for the Mentally Handicapped, *Services for the Mentally Handicapped in Hampshire*, Wessex Regional Health Authority, 1978, p. 33.

67 Crossman, R., *supra*, p. 411.

68 Allen, M. and Nicholson, M., *Memoirs of an Uneducated Lady*, Thames and Hudson, 1975, p.183.

8 Why the differences?

The enormous differences in the care offered to different groups of children unable to live in their own homes over the past thirty years must raise three questions.
- How was it that the reforms proposed by the Curtis Committee were so quickly taken up and so energetically implemented ?
- Why were some groups of children – particularly those with mental handicaps – excluded from the reforms ?
- Why has there been no agitation since on their behalf, strong enough to bring similar reforms in conditions which have often been as damaging to them, if not more so, as the orphanages were to the children in them before the war ?

At its simplest, it seems that no widespread social change is possible until enough people who know what they are talking about agree that a given situation must change. They then have to convince enough other people that change is needed: the 'problem' must become obvious to more than a selected few. Among these people must be enough who can actually do something about it, and this is not likely to happen unless the original advocates can suggest a solution which seems possible. Steps have then to be taken to make sure that their solution is enforced – for instance, by legislation. And finally, the original advocates and others they have picked up along the way have to keep pressing to ensure that what they hoped would happen actually does.

This section looks at the lead-up to and the immediate aftermath of the report of the Curtis Committee, the report of the Royal Commission on Mental Illness and Mental Deficiency (1957) and the Government White Paper *Better Services for the Mentally Handicapped* (1971). The second two have been chosen because they are milestones in the development of post-war policy towards mentally handicapped children and adults. As we shall see, the drive and clarity of the Curtis recommendations and the determined implementation of what the Committee wanted to see have not been repeated since.

Curtis—before and after

Even before the Curtis Committee was set up, there was widespread disquiet about the situation of children in care. Lady Allen of Hurtwood who knew about what was happening and about what should happen in well-run establishments – got what an Editor of *The Times* has called a 'staggering' response to her letter asking for a public enquiry into the 'largely uncivilised territory' of child care. 'Day after day and week after week the letters poured in. Many came from leaders in social work and others who also had first-hand experience. Even after the normal correspondence had been closed, *The Times* had to publish no fewer than six round-ups of further letters.' (1)

Lady Allen was also a skilled politician with influential political friends (Herbert Morrison, the Home Secretary of the time, later proposed marriage to her). Before her letter even appeared in *The Times*, she lined up people whose response to it would lend weight to her demand for an enquiry. Afterwards, she fed a spate of parliamentary questions to MPs and finally, 158 of them signed a request for an enquiry. The original *Times* letter had been published on July 15, 1944 ; the announcement of the enquiry was made on December 7. Even though Herbert Morrison said privately that he felt the case for reform had been overstated, (2) public interest was fanned by the death of Dennis O'Neill in foster care (see page 5).

If Morrison felt that the orphanages were not as bad as had been claimed, others, including people who had grown up in them, knew differently, and in *Whose Children ?* Lady Allen was able to draw on extensive correspondence in the provincial press as well as letters to her personally, to keep the pot boiling. When the Curtis Committee reported, she felt that its revelations 'made it impossible for the Government not to act on the recommendations'. Nevertheless, she knew 'it would be unsafe to leave the parliamentary process to take its natural course without continued vigilance. The effectiveness of parliamentary Government depends on sustained public interest and well-informed public criticism.' (3)

While Lady Allen threw herself into one of her other campaigns, there were enough outraged members of parliament to ensure that the Curtis Report got a proper hearing. The end of a war is traditionally a good time for major social investment in the country's future. So, school meals were introduced after the discovery of the poor shape of Boer War recruits ; so, the end of the First World War brought major educational legislation ; so, in 1944, the scope of public education had been extended. And so, when the King's Speech was found in 1946 to have no reference to the Curtis report, which had come out a month before, there was a generosity of MPs ready to champion the children. It would, said Mr Wilson Harris of Cambridge University, 'be absurd to expect so trifling a matter as the welfare of 125,000 children to take its place beside, for example, a measure of such domestic importance as one to enable local authorities to operate civic restaurants'. But, he went on, 'as long as 10% of children are undergoing the treatment depicted in this report, then I say we have a right to come here and call on the Government to undertake that it will take action'. (4) The motion to deplore the omission of legislation from the King's Speech was rejected, but a bill was in fact introduced in the following year and watched through all its stages by the vigilant Lady Allen. (5)

The Curtis Committee had not simply agreed that 'something had to be done'. It knew exactly what it wanted to see in the way of child care in future and its solutions were perfectly possible solutions. Boarding out was not a new concept by any means ; the Committee simply strengthened the safeguards in an already established system. Experience of residential nurseries during the war had shown that it was possible to offer children better care than they got in public assistance institutions. The Committee's views were widely shared – not least by the men and women who became the leaders of the new children's departments and were prepared to do battle with recalcitrant councillors. If Government had shown itself reluctant, first to have an enquiry at all and then to speed through legislation, once that legislation was passed there was a large body of support for it. As we have seen, the Home Office guidance in the early years of the new service was characterised by its complete clarity on the service's objectives and the energy with which these were pushed forward.

So reform was launched for the majority of children living away from their own homes. The Curtis Committee, however, as we have seen, took a very different line when it came to the minorities. And it was that line which was pursued with more or less vigour in the years to come.

The Committee saw the care of physically handicapped children living away from home as very largely outside its scope. Partly this was because it took a very wide view of what constituted 'medical aspects' of care. Partly perhaps it was less concerned for them than it was for the majority of children away from home because they had their own advocates and their own department to care for them. For a start, most were not 'in care' in the sense that orphans and others removed from home were. They were in boarding schools receiving education – a perfectly acceptable middle-class place to be – or they were in hospitals, receiving 'treatment' – another perfectly acceptable place to be. The Ministry of Education had a new mandate to look after the first group and the National Health Service was about to be formed to look after the second ; they were to be coherently taken care of, unlike the children in care who were scattered between Ministries so haphazardly that Lady Allen was led to ask *Whose Children ?*. Given this situation, the perfectly possible solution became more boarding schools for those physically handicapped children who could not live at home. This was the extension of a pattern already established before the war, for both them and other children now identified as falling into the categories needing special education. So, as we have seen, the number of special boarding schools grew, and, as we have seen too, the Ministry of Education took seriously the Curtis approach in its own examinations of the quality of life in these schools.

The only possible solution for mentally handicapped children, as far as Curtis was concerned, was to remove them into 'properly staffed homes and colonies'. Its failure to see them as *children*, to be offered the same care as others not living at home, was not unusual at this time. The shortage of institutional places at the end of the war, with many still lost to the Emergency Bed Service, seemed desperate, and to call for more instead of examining their suitability for the care of children was the common solution to this particular problem. According to Mr Wilson Harris in the first debate on the Curtis report, its revelations had raised feelings of 'horror, indignation and shame'. But the sympathy was selective and the Curtis Committee's revulsion at finding mentally handicapped children mixed in with others readily found its echoes. The report, said Mr Wilson Harris, raised 'haunting pictures of normal healthy children shut up with mental defectives ; in one case with a revolting mongolian child, in another with a hydrocephalic idiot behind a screen, in another, with a blind imbecile boy making hideous noises day and night'. (6)

Mentally handicapped children got their own debate at the end of 1946. Dr Morgan of Rochdale called services for them 'one of the problems concerned with child welfare which have been most neglected in this country'. Local education authorities were not responsible for them if they were 'ineducable' (severely mentally handicapped) ; the Home Office was responsible only when they became delinquent, and the Board of Control and local mental deficiency committees were doing nothing.

'These children cannot be boarded out, because foster parents will not take them. That is quite natural, because these children are ineducable, they cannot be trained and nothing can be done for them. They are absolutely brainless individuals, incapable of education, training or improvement in any way. It is unfair that they should be left in the hands of their parents to set a bad example at home... Let us insist that institutions be established where these children can be cared for, which have a special staff and a child psychiatrist in charge of them. Let us do something to ease the lives of these children, so that we may feel that the humanity of the country is not being lost and that these children are getting some comfort in an institution or home.' (7)

The official reply of the Ministry of Health was that Dr Morgan's view of the plight of severely mentally handicapped children was the 'most distorted and exaggerated case' that it had ever heard. (8) A couple of months later, the Minister himself was able to refer a questioner who pressed about the lack of accommodation for these children to the Curtis report, on which he put a somewhat idiosyncratic gloss : 'they consider that our treatment of mentally defective children is satisfactory'. (9) The Committee had, however, found less to complain of in the mental deficiency institutions it visited than in many other places. The scene was set for the huge expansion of child admissions in the 1950s, and there were few advocates either to join with Dr Morgan of Rochdale or to question his views. The medical establishment had far more important negotiations on its mind in the years leading up to the establishment of the NHS. The political parties, while they were concerned enough to discuss the situation of children in care in general, had little or nothing to say about children who were mentally handicapped. (10) The National Society for Mentally Handicapped Children did not, at this time, exist. The National Association for Mental Health, in its evidence to the Curtis Committee, did not mention mentally handicapped children at all, although it acknowledged the problems that 'backward' ones could cause in children's homes : 'They cannot sit and read and write in the evenings, they cannot read the hymns in church or follow the service and are therefore restless and seek diversion.' They advised special psychiatrically–supervised hostels for 'difficult' children. (11)

So the seal was set on very different approaches to mentally handicapped children and others living away from home. The identification with adults carrying the same label rather than with children had been ratified and the assumption that they did not need what other children needed in the way of attention and affection had been made. Both these proved exceedingly hard to shake off.

The Royal Commission—before and after

The next major opportunity to look at the care offered to mentally handicapped children away from home came when the Royal Commission on Mental Illness and Mental Deficiency was set up in 1954. By this time, two organisations were specifically concerned with these children : the National Association of Parents of Backward Children (later the National Society for Mentally Handicapped Children), and the National Spastics Society (later the Spastics Society), which has a particular interest in multiply-handicapped children. The first of these organisations had some 7000 members and the second, some 4500.

As early as 1951, Dr Brian Kirman, from Fountain Hospital, the largest in the country to cater specifically for mentally handicapped children, was saying that 'the decision to place a child in an institution on account of mental deficiency is *almost never* in the child's interest, but it may be in the interests of another child or in that of the parents themselves' [his italics]. (12) Neither the National Association of Parents of Backward Chidren nor the National Spastics Society, however, took anything like his line in their evidence to the Royal Commission. Neither was set to challenge the assumption that some children should be cared for in mental handicap hospitals, nor to criticise the present hospital regimes. Indeed, the National Association warned the Commission that the potential waiting list for hospital places could have as many as 25,000 names on it. These parents seemed unsure in the face of medical authority. When asked what discharge procedures should replace the complicated ones in the Mental Deficiency Acts, they felt that there should be some reserve power to prevent mothers from taking their children home from a hospital. (13)

In its evidence, the National Association urged far more opportunities for the training and education of children living at home − with responsibility for this passing to the Ministry of Education at a time considered 'desirable and practicable' − and greater support for families. Where residential care was needed, regional hospital boards should provide 'small homely hostels' for 'young children who are acceptable in day schools or occupation centres and who do not require nursing care but merely custody and supervision' and 'older children who have lived amenably at home and are quite acceptable in the community, possibly able to work and at least partly to support themselves'. If such hostels were set up, 'high-grade' children now in institutions could move to them and so free beds for more urgent cases. (14)

The National Spastics Society, in its evidence, was concerned first and foremost with proper assessment for children with cerebral palsy and the provision of special schools for them. It shared the concern about the space that 'high-grade' children took up in institutions, while 'low-grade' children were forced to wait for places. (15) Finally, the general theme was echoed by the National Association for Mental Health, which wanted hospital units for 'low-grade defectives' who needed 'nursing or special care' – although it had nothing to say on where these units should be sited – and hostels catering for adolescents and young adults. (16)

Here was a new principle in residential services for mentally handicapped children. Instead of there being only one alternative to the family home – the mental deficiency institution – there should in future be two, the hospitals and local or health authority hostels. There was a second new principle : the most handicapped children should be offered a *different* form of residential care to the more able. The Royal Commission took both these principles on board in its recommendations and they were enshrined in the 1959 Mental Health Act.

The debate on the Royal Commission's report – only the second on mental disorder in twenty-seven years, as one member pointed out – was hardly revolutionary in tone. 'While every effort must be made and will be made to keep these tragic patients in the community,' said another, 'we must nevertheless face the fact that the best atmosphere for many thousands of mentally ill and subnormal persons is that of a hospital, where their condition is understood and where they are cared for by people trained in mental illness who can be relied upon to deal with them sympathetically and wisely.' (17) The public confusion between mental illness and mental handicap (which the Mental Health Act was to exacerbate by dealing with the two together), together with a prevailing set of attitudes to mentally handicapped children were well illustrated in one member's contribution to the debate on the second reading of the Mental Health Bill. Mr Mallalieu spoke of the distress of parents with such children and the effects on other children in the family who are 'almost invariably deeply disturbed by the presence . . .of one so difficult to deal with, perhaps very similar to them in most respects and yet so different . . . Which of us has not seen the girl who has been ashamed to bring into her own house her own boyfriends for fear of what they might see of a brother or sister who is mentally deficient ?' He worried that as a result of the new Act, many mentally ill [sic] people would be let loose on their families from institutions. (18)

In spite of such reservations, the Mental Health Act was generally hailed as opening a new chapter in the care of people who had what were now known as 'mental disorders'. Yet the development of alternatives to the mental handicap hospitals, for adults as for children, was slow. In the hospitals themselves, standards by the end of the decade were officially acknowledged to be falling rather than rising. (19) The end of the decade saw a crisis in these places rather than the results of a coherent development of policy. There were three main reasons for this : the lack of political bite among voluntary societies most concerned ; the failure of these and their natural allies among professional workers to press for change ; and the quite extraordinary lack of leadership from the Ministry of Health.

None of the three main voluntary organisations concerned with mentally handicapped children in hospital gave indication to a wider public during the 1960s that conditions in these places gave cause for alarm. When James Loring, later director of the Spastics Society, wrote in 1966 that 'far too little regard' had been paid to the 'excellent work' being done for children who needed medical and nursing care in hospital, 'often in bad and overcrowded conditions', he was doing no more than reflecting a general tone. (20) When he had a radical change of mind two years later, and likened mental handicap hospitals to 'seventeenth century slave ships', the National Society for Mentally Handicapped Children (NSMHC) found this a 'wildly irresponsible extravaganza' – although subsequent revelations more than justified Loring's stand. The NSMHC, indeed, took something of a perverse pride in not meddling in political affairs. Its 1968 Annual Report was called *Down to Earth*, and it said of itself : 'The NSMHC is a down to earth organisation concerned... with the simple human problems... weekly transport to hospital, books for teachers, toys for toddlers'. (21) At this time, both the NSMHC and the National Association for Mental Health, as one observer commented, 'have traditionally chosen to be the sort of pressure group that nobbles the influential... and works behind the scenes, rather than the sort that exploits public relations, calls press conferences and denounces inadequacies in quotable rhetoric'. (22)

If the major voluntary organisations concerned did not, during the early 1960s, provide the strong advocacy needed if the residential care of mentally handicapped children was to improve, neither did they use such 'professional' concern as existed to press for change. The determined lobbying of the National Association for the Welfare of Children in Hospital offers a striking contrast. It drew on Bowlby's writing on maternal deprivation and James Robertson's series of Tavistock films on the same theme : no wonder the Ministry of Health issued so many circulars on the need for unrestricted visiting of sick children in hospital throughout this period.

So the NSMHC failed to seize on the findings of Tizard's Brooklands experiment, which it itself had sponsored, to educate a wider public on the need for change. In 1960, the initial findings were acknowledged and then dismissed in a Ministry of Health comment in a parliamentary debate on bringing severely mentally handicapped children into the educational system. The results of the Brooklands work were, the Ministry spokesman said, 'very satisfactory'. 'This was probably to be expected, for doctors generally would agree that the possibility of individual attention conferred by a high staffing ratio can achieve much for patients of this type. But inevitably limitations on capital programmes and the difficulties experienced in recruiting staff means that schemes of this sort, however good the results achieved, can at present have only a limited application.' (23) The most important of Brookland's implications – that severely mentally handicapped children flourished under a *child care* rather than a 'hospital' regime – was thus completely glossed over.

And if MPs had not been briefed to argue the importance of Brooklands, neither did it seem important to many people nearer the grass roots. Some workers and organisations did, however, take up the challenge. Meldreth, the Spastics Society unit for multiply-handicapped children, was set up in 1966 under the influence of the Brooklands findings. (24) A Fountain Hospital ward of Queen Mary's Hospital, Carshalton, to take another example, was set up in two family groups, with nursery education for the more able of its twenty children and 'systematic play' for the others. The results were not as dramatic as those of the original Brooklands. (25) But Maureen Oswin, at the end of the 1960s, found a ward only a stone's throw away from an experimental one, run on Brooklands lines, which was 'more like a storeroom for hospital beds, being kept clean and ready for some expected national disaster' than a home for children. One nurse she spoke to had worked on the experimental ward and found it not to her taste at all : 'The children got so much attention and were allowed to do as they liked and make a mess ; they started showing off and got ever so noisy and spoiled, really naughty they were.' (26) This lack of awareness of the need for change contrasts sharply with the support Lady Allen got for her letter to *The Times* from many people actually involved in child care.

If the lessons of the Brooklands experiment were not widely translated into practice, they nevertheless became important in the development of thinking about residential services to mentally handicapped children. From his results, Tizard suggested a completely different pattern of residential care for the future. He reckoned that thirty children in every population of 100,000 would need a place to live away from their family home and suggested that the most handicapped children – 'idiots' and those whose main need was for 'medical and nursing care' – should go to a long-stay annexe attached to a children's hospital. The rest – perhaps half of all the children – should go to hostels whch could be run by local authorities, be fostered or find a place in an ordinary children's home. (27)

In one sense, these proposals were something of a revolution : this was the first suggestion that in future no child should go to a mental handicap hospital, but that instead, all should be cared for within the context of general child health and welfare services. In another sense, the proposals were not revolutionary at all, but merely confirmed the principles adopted by the Royal Commission and enshrined in the Mental Health Act : that children with different degrees of handicap should be catered for in completely different ways. The divide in Tizard's plan between the children was clear. The 'idiots' in the long-stay annexes would be cared for by one permanent ward sister, under a paediatrician, while other staff worked on the ward for longer or shorter periods, 'either from interest or as part of their training'. 'The problems of recruiting nursing staff for the severely subnormal might be much eased if only a few dedicated women were to be asked to give their working lives to the nursing of idiots, while other nurses spent only occasional spells of duty with hopeless cases.' (28) So, while some mentally handicapped children would get the benefit of recognised child care practice, others would be offered perhaps a greater turnover than ever in the number of staff who cared for them, and in a completely different context of provision and staff-training.

Tizard's suggested categorisation of children as fit for one form of residential care or another was, as we shall see, to have wide-reaching effects on policy development right up until the end of the 1970s. A more radical practical development of his thesis has been the hostels developed by the Wessex Regional Hospital Board (now Health Authority) since the end of the 1960s. These have cared for children in the context of a hostel service to them and adults as well. They have gone further than Tizard proposed in 1964, by meeting the residential needs of *all* mentally handicapped children in given populations of 100,000 in twenty-place hostels, without distinction by degree of handicap. The children have done better than those in traditional hospital wards ; their contact with both their families and relevant professional workers has been greater too. (29)

In the period up to the end of the 1960s, however, the Ministry of Health was not making any such new proposals. In fact, it was not making many proposals at all. The extraordinary paucity of guidance on the hospital service to mentally handicapped people in general is a characteristic of the entire decade which followed the 1959 Mental Health Act. With few people to push it from behind, the Ministry of Health was able to indulge its sensitivity to the autonomy of the regional hospital boards to the full. When it did turn its attention to the mental handicap hospitals, in 1965, as we have seen, Tizard's suggestion that the most handicapped children could live in paediatric annexes found its way into the guidance, but could easily have been missed in the weight of general suggestions for children and adults alike. There was certainly nothing from this Ministry to match in determination and clarity the guidance from the Home Office in the early days of the children's service.

'Better services for the Mentally Handicapped'— before and after

If the 1960s was characterised by a general inertia about the state of the mental handicap hospitals and the children and adults forced to live in them, the 1970s has been characterised by almost continual debate about these places and alternatives to them. The change came abruptly, and it was brought about not by the voluntary societies, nor by the professional and research workers who might have been expected to push for reform, but by the Secretary of State for Social Services, however unwillingly, with the publication of the report on Ely Hospital, in Cardiff.

The report had arrived in the Ministry of Health in September 1968 and immediately, according to Richard Crossman's own version of the story, the civil servants and Geoffrey Howe, the chairman of the enquiry, joined battle on how much of it should be published, with the Department bidding for an edited version and Howe standing out for the full story. The battle had raged over three months and three versions when the report landed on Crossman's desk for a snap decision before he handed responsibility for health in Wales to the Secretary of State for Wales. 'I was furious, because it was outrageous to bring it to my notice on Monday night, giving me two days to agree with it, when I could have seen it at any time in the last three months.' Before he even read the report, Crossman decided that it would have to be published in full, or Howe would 'be entitled to go on television and talk about suppression'. Once he had read it, it became clear that it completely substantiated the allegations of malpractice at Ely which he had dismissed as 'outrageous' when he had first heard them. The report was duly published in full. (30)

The National Society for Mentally Handicapped Children and the National Association for Mental Health (NAMH) were both quick to claim that they had known about the conditions it revealed all along. 'Suddenly', said the NSMHC, 'all sorts of people were suddenly expressing concern and pontificating in all directions. Some people of course had known about this all the time and had been concerned and anxious about what was happening to subnormal people for many years, but no one listened.' (31) The NAMH put its own dilemma like this : 'How were we to break down the stigma which still attached to mental disorders and at the same time tell the truth about conditions in many of our mental hospitals ? Should we not be hitting at a devoted and hard-working profession if we said that overcrowding and understaffing were bidding fair to undermine the good picture of the mental hospital which undoubted advances in treatment had built up ?' (32)

There was little time, however, for this sort of justification. The Ely report was published in March 1969, and in September a major study of the conditions in mental handicap hospitals, for adults and children alike – commissioned by the National Society for Mentally Handicapped Children – was published to remove any last doubts that conditions at Ely Hospital had been an isolated unhappiness. (33)

By then, as we have seen, three major initiatives had been set in train : a programme of minimum standards in physical provision and staffing for mental handicap hospitals had been launched, to be achieved within five years ; the Hospital Advisory Service had been set up ; and a working party was looking at how the organisation of services could be improved – work which was eventually, after a change of government, to emerge as *Better Services for the Mentally Handicapped.*

It has been reckoned that never in the history of Britain or elsewhere had so much public attention and sympathy been turned to the needs of mentally handicapped people as came their way between 1969 and 1971. (34) There was a public revulsion against the deprivations of hospital life, fuelled by press and television reports. There was, as we have seen, a coincidental optimism about the possibilities of 'community care', in the wake of the Seebohm report. There was even official action. How, then, were the needs of mentally handicapped children for decent residential care still unmet at the end of the period ?

The first reason has to do with the way the scandal about hospitals arose when it did. The Ely report – as indeed the others into conditions in Farleigh, South Ockenden and Normansfield hospitals which followed it – was concerned with care for 'the mentally handicapped' as a group. The reforms proposed by the Department of Health were equally concerned with provision for this group of people. The fact that mentally handicapped children were *children* was not seen as demanding any particular response other than the reform of services to 'the mentally handicapped'. As we have seen, it was only towards the end of the period that the National Development Group and Jay Committee emphasised that these were chidren first and mentally handicapped second.

Secondly, scandal has ever been an unpredictable director of change and one initiative announced in the wake of the Ely Hospital enquiry was to create a confusion which has bedevilled reform ever since. While *Better Services for the Mentally Handicapped* proposed that the hospital populations should be halved, a programme to reach minimum standards in those hospitals had *already* been announced two years before. This approach to the very real problem of making life tolerable for people living and working in hospitals during the lengthy period of their run-down has in practice meant that money has consistently been poured into the hospitals, while alternative developments have suffered and the minimum standards had not, by the end of 1979, been universally achieved. The dilemma is not a new one. At the start of the children's service, the Home Office faced the equally pressing problem of improving conditions in large institutional orphanages while at the same time developing a new system of small group homes. As we have seen, its solution was clear. The 'minimum consistent with the well-being of the children' was to be put into structural alterations and the rest of available money into staff and furnishings, both of which could move to new buildings when these became available. The fact that old buildings were unsuitable was a reason not to pour money into them, but to increase boarding out. (35)

The Home Office advice worked because it and the local authorities both knew what kind of service they were aiming for. The DHSS programme of minimum standards, by contrast, was launched *before* there was any context of goals for the service as a whole. It was only in 1978, when the National Development Group tackled the problems of improving life in hospital that the confusion, for children at least, began to be sorted out; its recommendations for them had to do very much with the transferrable resources of staff and child care practices, and very little to do with the fixed ones of bricks and mortar. (36)

Peter Townsend, himself a close observer of the 'post-Ely' scene, has identified a third reason why the initiative for a radically new policy for mentally handicapped people was lost between 1969 and 1971. The talk of reducing hospital numbers, of increasing resources and staff in the community, he said, produced a 'classical reaction' from nursing staff and medical superintendents in the mental handicap hospitals.

'All that was required, they said, was better resources and an end to the hurtful smears which sapped morale and endangered staff recruitment. Far from being run down, the hospitals should be recreated and developed as centres of excellence, upon which the services for the community as well as the inmates could be based. Because so few staff work for the handicapped outside hospital and are so poorly organised, and because the nursing and medical staff are dominant inside these hospitals and can bring pressure to bear on the Department of Health through a range of committees, it is not surprising that they were so successful in opposing the announcement of a new kind of policy.' (37)

To this political pressure could be added others of a rather more negative kind. As the Court Committee pointed out, most paediatricians simply have not been properly trained in the social and educational aspects of handicap (38) – which might just have something to do with their reluctance to take up first Tizard's and then the Ministry of Health's suggestion that they should in future be responsible for the residential care of severely mentally handicapped children. Local authorities, as we have seen, hardly showed enormous enthusiasm for providing residential homes for mentally handicapped children in the decade after the Mental Health Act was passed. By the beginning of the 1970s it could seem that the only people who wanted to care for these children, other than their own families, were those who had them by tradition – the mental handicap hospitals.

When it eventually came, as we have seen, *Better Services for the Mentally Handicapped* allowed scope for all comers. It perpetuated the notion that the most severely handicapped children should be offered a different form of residential care to those with less serious handicaps – in hospitals rather than in residential homes. Some five years later, the official target figures for children in hospital were in shreds : there were already some 2000 fewer children in hospital than forecast for 1991. In spite of this, however, the official DHSS line by the end of the period was that there were still children who would need care in hospital.

The White Paper has left two major confusions in its wake. The first has to do with exactly what sort of hospital provision should be offered to mentally handicapped children. The list of options had proliferated bewilderingly since the mid-1960s. At the last count, it looked something like this :
- within existing large mental handicap hospitals ;
- administered by these hospitals, but on the edge of their site or off it altogether ;
- on the site of general hospitals, attached to their children's departments ;
- off the site of general hospitals, attached to their children's departments ;
- off the site of general hospitals, attached to their child psychiatry departments ;
- on the site of general hospitals which also have large units for mentally handicapped adults ;
- in new district mental handicap hospitals ;
- in specialist regional units.

The DHSS has not helped authorities make up their minds between these alternatives. The Wessex alternative has remained 'experimental'.

The second major confusion – which applies as much to adults as to children – has been over exactly which children need the services that only a hospital can provide and what, especially in the light of Maureen Oswin's 1978 study and the Jay Committee's recommendations, these services are. At worst, the confusion can lead to assumptions like that of a working party of the National Children's Bureau (then National Bureau for Co-operation in Child Care) in 1970, which concluded that there was an 'inadequate' number of hospital beds because there was a waiting list of some 1700 children. (39) Even the usually decisive Court Committee was unable to say how many residential places in a given population should be provided by health authorities and how many by social services departments. The DHSS call for an end to 'inappropriate' admissions has not resolved the confusion.

Given these two major confusions, it is hardly surprising that the most usual way out of them has been inaction. Local authorities have been extremely slow to provide residential homes. The health service has, with a few notable exceptions, not responded by setting up alternatives to traditional medical units ; it had either left the children where they were and made considerable investment in improving their environment, or planned for new 'small' hospitals which will cater for children and adults alike. In either case, it has become very selective in long-term admissions. Seven years after the White Paper, the net result has been that families have less recourse for the residential care of their mentally handicapped child.

Meanwhile, there has been no shortage of suggestions for the future. So the Royal Medico-Psychological Association (now the Royal College of Psychiatrists) suggested in 1972 that in-patient assessment units for both children and adults should be built up in existing mental handicap hospitals. (40) So the

101

National Children's Bureau in a 1972 review of the research on mental handicap concluded : 'These children [the most severely handicapped] need the maximum help from the various specialists – medical, paramedical and educational. To say that they are not adequately provided in the subnormality hospitals at present is no reason for saying that they cannot be provided. Such hospitals might be the best place to offer a concentration of specialists for the children who need them.' A comparison between this provision and paediatric units in general hospitals was 'essential'. (41)

The comparison has not been made and is not likely to be. To suggest such an injection of scarce resources into mental handicap hospitals, when there are already too few in the general community provision, seems to be quite simply a non-starter.

There has also been a plethora of suggestions designed to make hospitals not like hospitals at all. A very great deal of money has been poured into trying to turn wards into 'domestic-type' units. Other observers have seized on the components of care as well as its physical setting. So the National Children's Bureau said in 1970 : 'Subnormality hospitals may have to provide some residential care, but they do not necessarily need to be hospitals and nurses may not necessarily have duties associated with nursing physically ill or handicapped or mentally defective patients. Another approach, modelled on child care practices and homelike handling, could be incorporated, even in large institutions, to the great benefit of the child's development.' (42) As we have seen, very much the same approach was being taken by the National Development Group six years later. So the Council for Children's Welfare in 1975 suggested that the care of children in long-stay hospitals should be transferred to the local authority social services department ; care would then be given by child care staff. (43)

All these suggestions raise the same question. Why pour so much money and energy into creating facsimiles of the real thing ? If children can live in 'domestic-type' units, why can they not live in ordinary houses ? If care is to be 'modelled on child care practice', why can it not be provided by those who provide child care ? If local authorities are to run hospital wards, why can they not instead provide housing for the children now in those wards ?

In 1975, Campaign for the Mentally Handicapped urged that all mentally handicapped children who needed to leave their family homes, whatever their degree of handicap, should be cared for by local authority social services departments within the framework of their other child care services. (44) In 1978, it was the voluntary societies most concerned with mentally handi-capped children which offered what seemed the only sensible way out of the policy confusion. EXODUS, a campaign set up by the Spastics Society, the National Society for Mentally Handicapped Children, MIND (the National Association for Mental Health), Campaign for the Mentally Handicapped and Kith and Kids, urged that all mentally handicapped children now in hospital should be rehoused by their own local authority social services departments within four years, within the normal range of provision for children not able to live with their own families. This programme should be made mandatory on local authorities and met out of a specific grant. Once the programme was complete, no child at all would be living in a mental handicap hospital. Their children's wards would then close. (45) In 1979, the Jay Committee's model of care endorsed the view that no child should have to seek residential care in a mental handicap hospital.

But the children living in these hospitals and those with no other alternative to their family homes were still waiting for a change in official policy by the end of that year. For them, Curtis's unfinished business was still unfinished.

Notes

1 Allen, M. and Nicholson, M., *Memoirs of an Uneducated Lady*, Thames and Hudson, 1975, pp. 178–80.

2 *ibid.*, p. 184.

3 *ibid.*, p. 200.

4 *Hansard*, House of Commons, vol. 430, 765–72.

5 Allen, M. and Nicholson, M., *supra*, pp. 207–8.

6 *Hansard*, House of Commons, vol. 430, 765–72.

7 *ibid.*, vol. 431, 1569–72.

8 *ibid.*, vol. 431, 1573.

9 *ibid.*, vol. 432, 1928.

10 See, for instance, Donnington, H., *The Care of Homeless Children*, Fabian Society, 1948 ; Liberal Party Organisation, *Nobody's Children*, 1947.

11 Thomas, R., *Children without Homes*, National Association for Mental Health, 1946.

12 Kirman, B., in *Journal of Mental Science*, vol. 99, 1951, p. 531.

13 *Royal Commission on The Law Relating to Mental Illness and Mental Deficiency*, Minutes of Evidence, 4th Day, HMSO, 1954, oral questions 934–47.

14 *ibid.*, p. 156.

15 *ibid.*, Day 10, pp. 386–7.

16 *ibid.*, Day 12, pp. 467, 473.

17 *Hansard*, House of Commons, vol. 573, 46.

18 *ibid.*, vol. 598, 820.

19 *Better Services for the Mentally Handicapped*, DHSS and Welsh Office, Cmnd. 4683, HMSO, 1971, para. 90 *e.s.*

20 Loring J., 'Meldreth – a Pioneer Unit for the Training of Spastic Children', in *Special Education*, vol. 55, Spring 1966, p. 22.

21 National Society for Mentally Handicapped Children, *Annual Report*, 1968.

22 Nightingale, B., *Charities*, Allen Lane, 1973, p. 205.

23 *Hansard*, House of Commons, vol. 623, 1449.

24 Loring, J., *supra*, pp. 21 *e.s.*

25 Stephen, E. and Robertson, J., 'Can Institutional Care Improve ?' in *Special Education*, vol. 55, Winter 1966, pp. 13–16.

26 Oswin, M., *The Empty Hours*, Allen Lane, 1971, pp. 159–60.

27 Tizard, J., *Community Services for the Mentally Handicapped*, Oxford University Press, 1964, p. 79.

28 *ibid.*, pp. 169–70.

29 Kushlick, A., Palmer, J., Felce, D. and Smith, J., *Summary of Current Research in Mental Handicap Work*, Health Care Evaluation Research Team, Wessex Regional Health Authority, 1977.

30 Crossman, R., *Diaries of a Cabinet Minister*, vol. 3, Hamish Hamilton and Jonathan Cape, 1977, pp. 408, 410.

31 National Society for Mentally Handicapped Children, *Annual Report*, 1969.

32 National Association for Mental Health, *Annual Report*, 1969.

33. Morris, P., *Put Away*, Routledge and Kegan Paul, 1969.

34 Townsend, P., 'The Political Sociology of Mental Handicap', in *The Social Minority*, Allen Lane, 1973, p. 198.

35 *Work of the Children's Department. 6th and 7th Reports*, Home Office, HMSO, 1951 and 1955, para. 56 and para. 47.

36 *Helping Mentally Handicapped People in Hospital : a Report to the Secretary of State for Social Services by the National Development Group for the Mentally Handicapped*, DHSS, 1978.

37 Townsend, P., *supra*, p. 200.

38 *Fit for the Future : Report of the Committee on Child Health Services* (Court Report), Cmnd. 6684, HMSO, 1976, paras 14.14 and 14.77.

39 Younghusband, E., *et al* (eds), *Living with Handicap*, National Bureau for Co-operation in Child Care, 1970, p.183

40 Royal Medico-Psychological Association, 'Future Patterns of Care for the Severely Subnormal', in *British Journal of Psychiatry*, vol. 119, pp. 95–6.

41 Pilling, D., *The Handicapped Child*, National Children's Bureau, 1972, p. 81.

42 Younghusband, E., *supra*, p.196.

43 *No Childhood*, Council for Children's Welfare, 1975, pp. 15–16.

44 *Whose Children ?*, Campaign for the Mentally Handicapped, 1975.

45 *Manifesto*, EXODUS, 1978.

9 What next?

As we have seen, official attitudes to the care of handicapped children away from their own homes, especially in hospitals, have gradually been catching up with those accepted thirty years ago for children who are not handicapped. We are still, however, far from seeing that philosophy put into practice for handicapped children. We do not yet even have a framework of provision which is comparable to that offered to other children in search of a substitute home.

Many valuable suggestions, drawing on accepted child care practice, have been made on the quality of care that we should now be offering to mentally and physically handicapped children away from home. (1) The Jay Committee's model of care and proposals for staffing offer a strong basis for future action. This chapter tries to set a legal and administrative framework within which these recommendations can be implemented. Until all children away from home, whatever their degree of handicap, are brought into a common framework of provision, the discrimination which has dogged services for the most vulnerable of all will continue.

An end to the hospital as a 'home'
Children with mental handicaps

We have seen how the standards of child care in mental handicap hospitals in particular have remained, despite the recent exhortations for reform, quite appallingly low. We have seen how the very nature of hospital organisation militates against good child care practice. We have seen too that the very existence of hospitals as a resource for the *care* of chidren, rather than active medical treatment, has skewed our perceptions of those children and their needs, and discouraged local authorities from taking seriously the responsibilities they carry for all children who need a substitute home.

The notion that the most severely handicapped children need services which 'only a hospital can provide' has proved exceedingly hard to shake off. The furthest that the DHSS has gone towards admitting that hospitals are not proper places for children to live in, as we have seen, is a commitment to encouraging health and local authorities to end 'inappropriate' admissions. But exactly what constitutes such an admission has never been suggested, let alone argued through. Maureen Oswin's 1978 study makes a mockery of the claim that mental handicap hospitals at present provide services which could not be provided elsewhere for the most handicapped children ; indeed, it would be hard to provide fewer than those she found.

What is needed now is a ministerial directive that :
i. all children living in mental handicap hospitals will be rehoused within

the normal framework of local authority provision for other children not living with families, and this within a specific time-limit. Four years seems reasonable ;

ii. admissions to these hospitals of any child will cease by the same date ;

iii. children's wards in mental handicap hospitals will then close.

Children with physical handicaps

Although physically handicapped children living in hospital have not attracted nearly as much attention as those in mental handicap hospitals in recent years, their plight is similar and a similar approach is needed to bring them within the framework of the ordinary child care service. The Hospital Advisory Service has shown that, because of over-provision of paediatric beds, children are kept in hospital, or even admitted for social reasons, and tend to become 'long-stay' without anyone really noticing, when they do not need the services provided by a hospital.

What is needed now is a ministerial directive that :

i. all children living for more than four months in a non-psychiatric hospital will be reviewed by a joint health, social services and education team, within twelve months, and plans made for their future ;

ii. only those who can be shown to need active medical treatment will remain in hospital. The others will be found new homes within the normal range of provision for children away from their family within one year ;

iii. those who do remain in hospital will
  - live in special units jointly staffed by residential child care workers and nurses, under the overall charge of a child care worker and
  - be reviewed monthly by a multidisciplinary team including medical, nursing, social services and educational staff to plan for their future outside the unit.

The programme is a modest one. To bring all children out of mental handicap hospitals will mean, on average, that local authority social services departments the size of the city of Cambridge (100,000 population) will accept responsibility for only nine children more than they do at the moment. Each ESN(S) school, on average, will have to find only ten extra places. To bring all children who do not need active medical treatment out of non-psychiatric hospitals will mean a task about a quarter that size.

Yet clearly even such a modest programme will not succeed unless two things are guaranteed :

i. alternative homes – most children live in hospital because, for one reason or another, it has proved impossible for their families to have them at home ;

ii. extra finance for at least the period of transfer.

Alternative homes

While there is no evidence that some children need to live in hospital simply because of the extent of their handicap, there is a fair amount of evidence that even the most severely handicapped can live in settings which come within the normal range of what is offered to other children away from home. It should not be forgotten either that some children may indeed be able to return home, if, and only if, their parents are able to specify exactly what support they need to make this possible and are guaranteed that support. The help may include a home help, a forty-hour a week care worker, a live-in care worker who enables the rest of the family to take a break, respite care for the child away from the family home, at regular intervals as well as 'on demand' at moments of crisis. Clearly, though, there can be no question of forcing parents to have a child at home. Clearly, too, local authorities will have to be very sure about exactly what they can and cannot guarantee by way of support before they make any promises to parents.

Alternatives to the child's family home will include :

i. *Fostering.* This is the Jay Committee's first choice for mentally handicapped children who cannot live with their own families. The choice should not be denied to any handicapped child in search of a home. The Eastern Nebraska Community Office of Retardation offers a model of a highly successful fostering programme for children with mental handicaps and multiple ones as well, using what we would call 'professional foster parents'. The essential elements in its programme are training, decent pay and continuing support for the foster parents – including all the services which would normally be offered to a family with a mentally handicapped child. (2)

ii. *Adoption.* Parents for Children, a London-based agency, is showing that even children traditionally known to be extremely hard to place can find adoptive parents. These include children with physical or mental handicaps, or both. (3)

iii. *Ordinary children's homes.* We have seen that some children with physical or mental handicaps live in local authority children's homes with children who are not so handicapped. This is not usually, though, a very active policy. Dr Barnardo's North West Division has shown since the beginning of the 1970s that an active policy of welcoming often very severely handicapped children into its homes presents few problems to staff or children, and makes for often dramatic development among the handicapped children. (4) The Jay Committee points out that if this form of care is to be successful, it will require attention to the needs of the group which the handicapped child will join and to the skills and interest of residential care staff. It believes, however, that 'increasingly children of all degrees of handicap could be accommodated in the normal provision of residential care for children provided by statutory and voluntary agencies'. (5) What it says about children with mental handicaps applies to those with physical disabilities as well.

iv. *Specialist children's homes.* This has been the alternative most often chosen by local authorities for mentally handicapped children at least, although they have been slow to welcome severely and multiply-

107

handicapped children and, as we have seen, there are far too few homes.

Two agencies have shown how small, specialist homes can help the most severely handicapped. The London Borough of Islington, in co-operation with the local health authority, has set up Field End House specifically for such children, together with provision of 'on demand' places for others who live with their own families. (6) Dr Barnardo's North West Division has gone further than this by using *ordinary* housing in Skelmersdale for a small number of children, with 'satelite' units where two children live with two members of staff. This service, which draws on the experience of the Eastern Nebraska Community Office of Retardation, illustrates two very important points. Ordinary housing can be used for even the most handicapped children, and it is possible to provide homes for a small group of children instead of the twenty or so usually housed in purpose-built local authority units. The Jay Committee, as we have seen, underlines the importance of this approach in its recommendation that specialist homes should be small and local to the children's own family.

v. *Special boarding schools.* As we have seen, this has been a major resource for physically handicapped children not able to live in their family homes. These schools have often been able to welcome children with very severe handicaps. Maureen Oswin found in her 1971 study that some of the children in the special schools she visited were just as handicapped as some of the children forced to live in hospital wards. When local education authorities are brought clearly into the system of review of children now living in non-psychiatric hospitals, it should be possible to find places in special boarding schools for some of these children, and to guarantee them the interest of social services departments.

Special boarding schools have provided fewer opportunities for children with mental handicaps. The National Development Group has recommended that the Secretaries of State for Social Services and Education should consider how these opportunities can grow. This should be done as a matter of urgency and guidance issued to both education and social services authorities.

The most severely handicapped children

Children with very severe disturbances of behaviour in addition to their mental handicap, or with extremely severe mental and multiple handicaps, it is often said, need special provision of their own. The National Development Group and the Jay Committee have suggested that special regional units may be set up for these children. These would not, however, be seen as part of the pattern of long-term residential care : they would be treatment units, whose aim would be to return the child to his or her own home, whether that is a family home or another.

As the Jay Committee pointed out, there is very little evidence that concentrating these children helps them more than dispersing them in alternative homes which welcome children with a range of abilities and brings in specialist help as necessary. Indeed, all the alternatives outlined above show that this pattern *can* work for all children, no matter how handicapped. The Eastern Nebraska Community Office of Retardation, in particular, found that it was simply creating trouble for children and itself when it set up a specialist home for the most disturbed children of all. It disbanded the home and the children are now progressing far better in foster homes and very small, mixed-ability children's homes.

If regional units are set up, the same rules should apply to them as to hospital units catering for children who need specific treatment because of their physical handicap. Each child should be reviewed monthly by a multi-disciplinary team and plans made for his or her future when the services of the unit will no longer be needed. The units should be staffed by people trained in the Jay pattern, with additional expertise brought in as necessary.

Finance

These alternatives will not be provided within the time-limit set by the Secretary of State unless special funding is available. The National Development Group (NDG) has identified three main sources of finance – in the context of enabling both children and adults to leave mental handicap hospitals : (7)

i. *Joint-financing.* This programme has provided some useful initiatives for mentally handicapped children in particular. As important, perhaps, it has helped to make joint-planning between health and social services departments a reality. The programme is extremely small, however, with competing claims on the resources it has. But the mechanism could be used for joint initiatives in future – like the units for physically handicapped children who need specific medical treatment and, possibly, regional units.

ii. *Earmarked funds.* The NDG was clear that some system of transferring earmarked funds from the hospital to the local authority service was essential. The principle is absolutely correct and the DHSS should now be working out how this can be done to fit in with rate support grant. There can be no question of allowing the problems of introducing this new method of financing to hold up the transfer of children from hospital. We pay departmental staff to solve such problems.

iii. *A central pool of funds.*   This is an alternative scheme to the one of earmarking funds. The funds would be held by either regional or area health authorities and used by local authorities to provide homes for people now in hospital.

A legal and administrative framework

We have seen how, at the moment, physically and mentally handicapped children living away from home may come under completely different Acts of parliament and regulations from those which protect other children in the same situation. A second level of reform, then, must be to ensure that all children living in alternative homes have the same degree of protection, whatever category they have been placed in.

Children with mental handicaps

The Harvie Committee (1974) made some detailed and urgent recommendations for changes in the law covering mentally handicapped children in residential care – particularly those in private and voluntary homes. (8) These have still not been acted on.

Three of the recommendations in particular seem no less urgent now than they did when they were first made.

i. Children who are not technically 'in care' but have been placed by social services authorities in private and voluntary homes should be covered by the Boarding Out Regulations 1955. This would give them the same degree of supervision and protection as is offered to children fostered by the local authority.

ii. Children placed privately by their parents should have the protection of the Children Act 1958. This gives the person who takes charge of them the duty to notify the social services department and that department the duty to visit and make sure the child is receiving satisfactory care.

iii. The regulations which cover homes for mentally handicapped children should be amended to provide the same protection for their inhabitants as the Community Homes Regulations do for theirs.

These recommendations may be only the start of the reform that is needed. Social workers are not themselves convinced that these three rubrics are completely satisfactory for the children in care they cover at the moment. Mentally handicapped children have the added disability of being covered by the Mental Health Act 1959, now under review. A first essential is to bring them out from under the provisions of that Act.

What is extraordinary is that the DHSS has shown no public signs at all that it has even considered the Harvie recommendations, far less done a thorough study to see if the protection they would provide is the best that can be done. The Department can act when it wants to – as witness the spate of circulars about an administrative framework for coping with child abuse and the amendments to the Children Act 1975 that came in the wake of the death of Maria Colwell. Amendments to the law covering mentally handicapped children in residential care must be made. The Harvie Committee, after all, was set up because a child died.

Children with physical handicaps

As we have seen, special residential schools have provided the main resource for physically handicapped children not able to live with their own families. One theme of this report has been how very little is known about the residential care – as opposed to the education – they are offered. Part of the reason for this must be that these schools are covered by educational rather than child care legislation and regulations. The Harvie Committee saw the advantages of dual registration – as a home and a special school – for those homes for mentally handicapped children which became schools under the Education Act 1970.

The DHSS and DES should examine how far this principle of dual registration should be applied to all special residential schools. This is particularly important in the light of the Warnock Committee's recommendation that each school should have a deputy head who is in charge of residential care.

Making the reforms work

Planning

Clearly, the business of offering a new chance to children now living in hospital will involve many agencies. This means that we need both joint-planning at local level and co-ordination in particular of the social services contribution, as this will be the main one in the new pattern of service.

i. Existing joint-planning machinery should be strengthened and a clear duty should be laid on joint-planning teams to achieve the reforms within the specified time-limit.

ii. The DHSS regional planning machinery for children in the care of local authorities has so far failed almost completely to work for children who may need care in specialist homes. Its remit should be extended to cover categorically children who are not technically 'in care' but nevertheless need a substitute home.

Monitoring

There is at present a plethora of monitoring bodies and none of them have worked well enough for children living in hospital or, indeed, at all for children in private and voluntary homes. Once children now in hospital are unambiguously in homes provided by local authorities, their care will be monitored by the Social Work Advisory Service of the DHSS. Children in special schools, however, will, unless these schools are also registered as homes, still be monitored only by the education inspectorate whose concern is not with residential care. Meanwhile, the National Development Group has recommended that a full-fledged inspectorate be set up to cover all services for anyone who is mentally handicapped and with the power to ensure that its recommendations are acted on.

In all this, the important thing to ensure is that children with handicaps are guaranteed the attention of people whose first concern is with the care of children, rather than services to a particular group of children and adults.

i. The Social Work Advisory Service should take over responsibility for mentally handicapped children in residential care, whether they are now in hospital or elsewhere, drawing on the expertise of the National

Development Group, and any inspectorate that may be set up for mental handicap.

ii. Discussions should be held between the DHSS and the DES to see if the Service should also visit special boarding schools, pending a decision on dual registration of these schools.

Advocacy

The Court Committee had some strong things to say about the need for a strong advocate for children. The Children's Committee which was set up as a result of its proposals has been fairly silent since it started work. Some body is needed to urge reforms, to keep an outside check on their progress and above all, perhaps, to orchestrate local endeavour which tries to ensure a fair deal for handicapped children.

Is the Children's Joint Committee capable of doing this job ?

These recommendations will take energy and even some courage to implement. They will be only the start of a decent service to children who are now often among the most deprived in the country. But they will at least lay the foundations of a service which clearly asserts that these children have the same rights as any others who cannot live in their own homes. They will signal an end to the discrimination against them which was endorsed by the Curtis Committee and has been accepted by every government since. And then a story of policy failure which has lasted thirty years and more will finally be brought to an end.

Notes

1 See especially, Oswin, M., *Children Living in Long-Stay Hospitals*, Spastics International Medical Publications/Heinemann Medical, 1978 ; *Helping Mentally Handicapped People in Hospital : A Report to the Secretary of State for Social Services by the National Development Group for the Mentally Handicapped*, DHSS, 1978.

2 Thomas, D., Firth, H. and Kendall, A., *ENCOR – A Way Ahead*, Campaign for the Mentally Handicapped, 1978.

3 Parents for Children is at 222 Camden High Street, London NW1.

4 Dr Barnardo's is at 7 Lineside Close, Liverpool L25 2UD.

5 *Report of the Committee of Enquiry into Mental Handicap Nursing and Care* (Jay Report), Cmnd. 7468-I, HMSO, 1979, para. 113.

6 Islington Social Services Department is at 17 Islington Park Street, London NI.

7 National Development Group, *supra*, paras. 1.2.7–1.2.13.

8 *Mentally Handicapped Children in Residential Care : The Report of a Study Group appointed by the Secretary of State for Social Services*, HMSO, 1974.

Appendix

Summary of main legislation and official reports which have affected children living away from home, 1948–79

1948   **Children Act :** set up children's departments within local authorities, under Home Office which also became responsible for voluntary children's homes ; gave local authorities duty to return children to their own homes whenever possible.

1955   **Report of the Committee on Maladjusted Children,** Ministry of Education : recommended that house staff in special boarding schools should be trained in child care.

1957   **Royal Commission on Mental Illness and Mental Deficiency :** recommended abolition of Board of Control and assumption of its powers by Regional Hospital Boards and local health authorities ; stressed need for greatly increased 'community care'.

1959   **Report of the Committee on the Welfare of Children in Hospital** (Platt Committee), Ministry of Health : stressed the importance of caring for children's emotional needs in hospital, recommended unrestricted visiting and provision for mothers to live in with their children.

1959   **Mental Health Act :** abolished Board of Control, brought mental illness and mental handicap hospitals under regular NHS hospital management and gave local health authorities powers to provide day and residential services for children and adults ; gave the majority of patients 'voluntary' rather than 'detained' status.

1963   **Children and Young Person's Act :** gave local authorities extended powers to help children at home.

1968   **Report of the Committee on Local Authority and Allied Personal Social Services** (Seebohm Committee), Home Office, Ministry of Health, Department of Education and Science, Ministry of Housing and Local Government : recommended new social services department in local authorities to take over duties of children's and other welfare departments.

1969   **Children and Young Person's Act :** brought together provision for children in need of care and children in trouble with the law in single local authority system of care.

1969   **Report of the Committee of Enquiry into Allegations of Ill-Treatment of Patients and other Irregularities at the Ely Hospital, Cardiff :** revealed not only specific abuses but a failure of the whole system of caring for mentally handicapped people.

1970   **Local Authority Social Service Act :** set up local authority social services departments, to take over existing local welfare provision, including day and residential care for mentally ill and handicapped children and adults and services of children's departments.

1970   **Education Act :** brought severely mentally handicapped children into the scope of education legislation for the first time ; schools for them to be categorised ESN(S).

1971   **Report of the Farleigh Hospital Committee of Enquiry :** further indications that all was far from well in mental handicap hospitals.

1971   **Better Services for the Mentally Handicapped,** Department of Health : plans for the development of services to mentally handicapped people over the next twenty years, including the reduction of hospital places for adults by about a half, but for children by about a seventh, and a corresponding rise in community services.

1972   **Report of the Committee on Nursing :** recommended new structure for the training of nurses and a new breed of 'care staff' to care for mentally handicapped children and adults.

1974   **Report of the Committee of Enquiry into South Ockenden Hospital :** more revelations about mental handicap hospital life.

1975   **Children Act :** for the first time, enshrined in law the principle that the welfare of the child must come first in adoption and care cases ; the wishes and feelings of the child to be taken into account as far as practicable ; strengthened the powers of local authorities over children in care ; strengthened the powers of foster and adoptive parents.

1976   **Education Act :** Section 10 laid down that in future handicapped children should be educated in ordinary, not special schools, except where this was impracticable, incompatible with the efficiency of the school or would involve unreasonable public expenditure.

1976   **Report of the Committee on Child Health Services** (Court Committee) : proposed an integrated child health service, to cover handicapped as well as non-handicapped children, including district handicap teams to help families with a handicapped child at home.

1978   **Report of the Committee of Enquiry into the Education of Handicapped Children and Young People** (Warnock Committee) : proposed extension of concept of special educational need to cover one in five of school population ; recommended abolition of statutory categories of handicapped child but retention of special schools for some children, including boarding schools.

1979   **Report of the Committee of Enquiry into Mental Handicap Nursing and Care** (Jay Committee) : proposed a common training for staff working in health and social services facilities, leading to a Certificate in Social Service in the care of adults or children. Also proposed a model of care which would ensure that all mentally handicapped people, whatever their degree of handicap, could get the residential and other services they needed within a generic framework and in their own locality.